HOPE FOR THE SECOND GENERATION

HOW IMMIGRANT CHILDREN CAN HELP REKINDLE CHRISTIANITY IN THE WEST

Tesfai Zeleke Tesema

with Ken Yoder Reed

TENTHPOWERPUBLISHING
www.tenthpowerpublishing.com

Interior design by Inkwell Creative
Cover design by Bemnet Yemesgen

Softcover ISBN: 978-1-938840-50-0
e-book ISBN: 978-1-938840-51-7

10 9 8 7 6 5 4 3 2 1

In my years as the supervisor of the Ph.D. in Missiology program at Concordia Theological Seminary, Fort Wayne, Indiana, we had several students from around the world who wrestled with what it means to raise their children in America. Particularly, what does it mean for their identity, and especially for their identity as a child of God? Tesfai Tesema systematically went about studying this issue for his dissertation, *Global Nomads: Identity and Assimilation of 1.5 and Second-generation Ethiopians in the United States*, which he successfully defended in February of 2009. But Dr. Tesema is not merely an academic. He is an experienced practitioner as a refugee himself, as a man, who with his wife Abeba, raised 1.5 and second-generation children, and who has a rich background in ministry to first, 1.5, and second-generation families. His book, which gratifyingly made much use of his dissertation research, doesn't simply describe the challenges immigrants and refugees have in raising children in a culture that is usually vastly different than their own. Rather, it is a *hopeful* book that brings the experiences of these families to life with a great deal of narrative. Moreover, this book shows how, despite the challenges, being raised as a bicultural kid is a wonderful gift from God to a new generation of people who will be uniquely equipped to bring understanding, help, healing, and the gospel to a world that is too torn by strife, racism, ethnocentrism, anger, and misunderstanding. Thank you, Dr. Tesema, for this very *helpful* contribution to understanding our contemporary world and for giving us *hope* as God continues to work in it through the children of immigrants and refugees.

Douglas L. Rutt, Ph.D.
Provost, Concordia Seminary
St. Louis, Missouri

Though the Ethiopian Diaspora is increasing exponentially, it is a subject that is little explored. The fact that the Ethiopians in the Diaspora are recent immigrants may account for lacuna. Migrants coming to new countries experience differential transactions, a process which leads to a reconfiguration of identities. Hybrid identity, a product of contested, dynamic, and negotiated selfhood impinging upon the realm of faith and belief systems. Global diasporas and migration are God's ways of expediating the fulfillment of the Great Commission around the world. Recognizing this reality is critically important for faith communities across the board as the center of global Christianity and the mission fields have shifted.

Tapping on his own broad life encounters, rich experiences, and viewing the phenomenon through the lens of years of pastoring immigrant churches, the author examines the real challenge 1.5 and 2.0 generation immigrants grapple with in navigating the intertwined spheres of their ethnic culture and the American culture. He explores the issue of how global Diaspora shapes the ecclesiological, theological, missional praxis of host societies. More importantly, he seeks to demonstrate the creative potentials and new opportunities the situation offers for the church of the Western hemisphere to rekindle its mission and avert trending towards decline. Dr. Tesema highlights this truth by way of reminding the churches in the West to pay attention and listen to the marginal voices in their neighborhoods with the aim of thinking afresh and reassessing their missional approaches in a moving, borderless world.

Hope for the Second Generation is a provoking and well-written contemporary account of the global Diaspora migration and how God is moving uniquely to accomplish his purpose in history by bringing the African factor as a multicultural and multilinguistic missional force and strain into the equation.

Dr. Tibebe Eshete
Michigan State University, History Department/
Department of Religious Studies

I ran into Dr. Tesema in mid 2000s when we were both studying at Ft. Wayne Seminary for our doctoral studies. Very quickly, I came to realize the depth and passion of Dr. Tesema as he wrestled among key issues that are relevant to the 1.5 and 2.0 second generation. Not only specific to the Ethiopia demographic, but he went far beyond by being inclusive of others. I have seen him conduct lots of workshops and research, which today makes him a distinguished scholar, pertaining to the second generation of immigrants who often are in opposition to their parents' culture and ways of life. Dr. Tesema has examined the depth of these issues.

Thus, it is my esteem pleasure as a fellow scholar in my own area of studies to encourage as many first-generation immigrant Christians and non-Christians, including other ethnic groups, to read such a distinguished scholar's book to enhance how they can deal with the 1.5/2.0 generation, whom often are in identity and cultural crisis. This 1.5/2.0 generation are the hope of all that we value as Christians in North America. Soon they will be taking over responsibilities from their first-generation parents. Thank you, Dr. Tesema, for such a distinguished scholarship and yet practical approach to the second generation. I endorse this book quite highly for the sake of the kingdom.

> **Rev. Dr. John Loum, M.A. Oxford, UK, M.A. Hartford Seminary**
> **Ph.D. in Islamic Studies Concordia Seminary, Fort Wayne**
> **Former Director, Ethnic Immigrant Institute of Theology at**
> **Concordia Seminary, St. Louis; Recipient, Distinguished Hoosier**
> **and Jefferson Award**

Every Christian parent and grandparent hopes a vibrant faith would lodge in the hearts of their children. Planting and nurturing faith in the next generation is a humbling challenge for any parent, but especially for a diaspora population. No one understands the generational and cultural differences facing the immigrant church better than Dr. Tesema. He has ministered to this population for decades. He mentors 1.5 and 2.0 generation leaders. He knows the aching desire to empower the next generation, first as a parent and now as a grandparent. Through it all, he remains curious and teachable. Find a friend, as you travel these pages, who loves the next generation and supports and equips their present and future faith and ability to lead.

> **Reverend Mike Lange**
> **President, California Nevada Hawaii District – LCMS**

Hope for the Second Generation discusses the real challenge 1.5 and 2.0 generation immigrants have in navigating the American culture and how God is using them to create a whole new future for an authentic, interethnic Christian community. Dr. Tesema draws these important conclusions based on his research findings that have positive implications for both members of immigrant churches and their American hosts. In so doing, he reveals the significant plan through which God is working through 1.5 and 2.0 generation immigrant individuals to revive the Western Church. This is a book every church leader who is part of a homogenous church needs to read.

> **Rev. Dr. John R Denninger**
> **President, Southeastern District – LCMS**

As a pastor who ministered to people making a transition from a foreign country to the United States, I can affirm how important this book is for all who are faced with similar circumstances. Good research was done, and helpful insights are given.

> **Dr. Norbert Oesch**
> **Former Executive Leader, Pastoral Leadership Institute (PLI)**

Hope for the Second Generation is an inspiring book written with passion and concern for second generation immigrants and their call to serve Our Lord Jesus Christ in Diaspora. The rich and practical stories shared in this book are followed with tactful approaches that will help parents, teachers, leaders, and anyone in ministry to find a path forward. The insight and perspectives narrated in the book has proved to be valuable for the International Ethiopian Evangelical Church where I serve as a senior pastor. Pastor Tesema's guidance and coaching has directly led to the establishment of Overflow Church, a second-generation church plant in downtown Silver Spring, Maryland, which you will read about in the book. I cannot recommend this book enough to first generation church leaders!

Pastor Dr. Hanfre Aligaz
Senior Pastor, International Ethiopian Evangelical Church
Washington, DC

We first met Tesfai at a PLI learning community a half dozen years ago. It didn't take either of us long to realize that we had plenty to learn from this man and his story. Since that time we've taught together. Laughed together. Dreamed together. Had Ethiopian coffee ceremony together with he and his wife, Abby, in their home in San Francisco. You'll be blessed and encouraged by every page in this book. It's rooted in rich experience as a refugee who came to meet Jesus. Tesfai is a pastor, teacher, consultant, trainer, and leader like few others. He travels extensively in the U.S and across the globe bringing what he's packaged here in these pages for you. We are pleased to call Tesfai our friend but more pleased that a lifetime of wisdom, biblical scholarship, and experience is offered here!

Gail Ficken
Founder/President, Multipli
Jock Ficken, Co-Executive Leader, Pastoral Leadership Institute (PLI)

Jesus told his disciples they would be his witnesses to the ends of the earth. For Jesus, America would have been just that. And Jesus is keeping his promise. Dr. Tesema shows the vitality of the church among new missionaries to America and in particular to the open door to reach their children. His insights on why and how to do this are important to anyone who wants to bring Christ to young people searching for their identity in a new culture.

Dr. Robert Scudieri
President, Mission Nation Publishing

Dr. Tesema has blessed the Body of Christ with this extremely helpful guide in increasing, empowering, and involving the second generation in the missional tasks of the Church. Second-generation immigrants at times have questions, seeking a guided response. This book is a perfect tool to serve that purpose.

Rev. Dr. Yonas Yigezu
President, Ethiopian Evangelical Church Mekane Yesus

What a gift to read and learn from Tesfai's book. Through the sharing of personal experience, profound insights from God's Word, in-depth research, stories, and examples of where the truths and principles Tesfai shares are being lived out and embodied, this book will provide a tremendous resource and contribution to the reaching of 1.5 and 2.0 generations within the USA and around the world! And not only of Ethiopians, but of those "elected strangers" that God has chosen, raised up, and is moving through from all nations and backgrounds, for His sake and for the sake of His Mission!

Dr. Scott Rische
Director, Pastoral Leadership Institute International (PLI)

Dr. Tesema's book is the result of soul searching and fascinating research, affirming the relevance of the gospel to the different generational needs today while strongly challenging the methods used to reach them. He beautifully describes the joy and pleasure of having diaspora children and the pain and frustration of raising them in a different culture. The affirmation one gets from this confrontation is that the gospel still redeems and that culture must be redeemed by exploring and applying different methods to challenge and persuade people to accept the salvation that is in Jesus Christ Our Lord. Simply put: Doctrine must stand; methods should change. May the Lord help us to remain humble and flexible to apply the principles mentioned in this book and continue to be salt and light in this world.

Dr. Betta Mengistu
President, Beza International Ministries
Addis Ababa, Ethiopia

One of the urgent responsibilities for our generation is to have a redeeming message for our children. Dr. Tesema, who is a pastor himself, has deeply investigated missiological, cultural, and racial matters in this important book, which every concerned Christian believer should read and have in his or her library. I applaud Dr. Tesema for his monumental work that is truly beneficial for the Body of Christ now and tomorrow.

Rev. Dr. Tolesa Gudina
Senior Pastor, Ethiopian Evangelical Church
Atlanta, Georgia

Hope for the Second Generation is a well-written landmark book addressing the compelling and profound potential and needs of the second generation. It will not only inspire and equip the 1.5 and 2.0 generations, but also calls first-generation church leaders and host culture missionary-minded Christians to consider the calling and potential of the 1.5 and 2.0 generation children as a God-given opportunity to rekindle Christianity in the West. A must-read book for all.

Pastor Dr. Zelleke Alemu
Veteran Church Planter

This book is an engaging, practical, and inspiring first-hand experience and academic exploration of the complexities of the immigrant church in America. It is also deeply personal. Pastor Tesfai shares his story and the stories of others who have wrestled with the "silent exodus" of 2nd generation immigrant children from the Christian church. Throughout, he challenges us to encourage and empower them so that, as they grow in their faith, they won't leave the church; they'll lead it and transform it.

Rev. Aaron Putnam
City Director, LINC San Francisco Bay Area

This book is replete with inspirational information devoted to immigrant children serving as missionaries to the world. The author's remarkable strategies make this book a must-read for every mission-minded individual. Therefore, as a called pastor who served as national missionary of The Lutheran Church – Missouri Synod, I highly recommend this prepared, cutting-edge, and groundbreaking research book.

The Reverend Philip S. Saywrayne
Senior Pastor, Christ Assembly Lutheran Church and
Missionary-at-Large
The Lutheran Church-Missouri Synod, New York State

Dr. Tesema continues to be one of the most effective missionaries to North America. His experience as a refugee from Communist Ethiopia in the 1970s who came to faith in exile through the testimony of faithful immigrant missionaries has prepared him with unique insight into the challenges of mission to immigrants and their children. Furthermore, as a church planter, he has faced the compounded challenges of ministering to the second generation of the churches he planted. *Hope for the Second Generation*, an outcome of his experience as a church planter and doctoral research, is a strong voice for strategic mission and ministry to the second generation. His multiethnic multicultural church planting vision will challenge church planters, mainstream and immigrant congregations, and denominational leaders. It is a book that is accessible to the common person and challenging to the theologian and field practitioner.

Rev. Dr. Yohannes Mengsteab
Mission and Ministry Facilitator, Texas District – LCMS

In a very clear and crisp way, author and practitioner Dr. Tesfai Tesema takes up a key question when it comes to missions and church planting today. How do we reach immigrant children who are drifting away from the church of their parents, and might the answer provide a clue for the health of the entire North American church of today? He addresses the question so many churches struggle with in our post-Covid world: "Do we come together to preserve our culture, or to grow together as multiplying disciples in our post-Christian culture?" His challenge to launch new churches that minister to immigrant children, as well as all children of our generation, must be heeded by all first-generation pastors and parents, as well as by leaders of every Anglo church in every community with diverse cultures. Providing solid Biblical and tested real-life case studies, Dr. Tesema helps us to see how the scattering of immigrants from the Global South is God's plan to call the West back to an authentic Christian faith and life. This book will have significant impact for those attempting to provide leadership on the North American mission field!

Rev. Dr. Peter A. Meier
Executive Director, Missions and Outreach
Florida Georgia District – LCMS

Dr. Tesema's story of immigration and the cultural challenges of second-generation immigrant Christians has great relevance for anyone concerned about the Lord's Great Commission and the future of Christianity in America. Like many immigrants and refugees who arrive on America's shores, Dr. Tesema's story could be made into a movie. His flight from Ethiopia and conversion to Christ in Saudi Arabia, followed by evangelistic and pastoral ministry in Sudan and later in the United States, give us a fascinating snapshot of how God is at work around the world and across multiple cultures in the space of a single life. His own story and the stories he shares of second-generation young people give us a glimpse into issues of racial and ethnic identity, as well as issues all young people wrestle with as they seek meaning and belonging in our society today. His book also provides insight into the problems faced by immigrant congregations as they seek to pass on the faith to a younger generation that has acculturated to the culture of the United States and has difficulty finding a spiritual home in the immigrant congregations of their parents. In a society of rapid social change, the problem of intergenerational cross-cultural discipling is relevant to all Christians, whether they are immigrants or not. I highly recommend this interesting and readable work for anyone who seeks to contribute to the work of God's multicultural Kingdom.

Dr. Eric J. Moeller
Pastor and Sociologist, Trinity Lutheran Church
Portland, Oregon

Hope for the Second Generation is conceived out of quite a deeper passion and many years of labor and is geared toward fulfilling a noble missionary cause and vision. I congratulate my good friend Tesfai for accomplishing the task that has been bubbling in his heart for a long time and also providing it for all of us. The first generation and our children are deeply grateful to his contribution to our Lord's Kingdom and particularly to our inter-generational community of faith! The book offers a profoundly relevant and groundbreaking work on the life transitions, struggles, and triumphs of an emerging generation of Christians and missionaries in the United States and beyond. I strongly recommend it for educators, pastors, and mission leaders to use it and join its appeal in changing the world through the fresh voices of the gospel!

Rev. Yared Halche, Ph.D.
Office of Mission Engagement
Southeastern District, LCMS Northern Region

Right on point! I wish I had this book in my hands several years ago. Dr. Tesema does an outstanding job presenting the reality and dynamics of the 1.5 and 2.0 generations of immigrants in the U.S., as well as the biblical principles and opportunities for these new generations to become the pioneers of the Multicultural Church movement.

Rev. Lincon Guerra
Texas District Mission Executive, LCMS

This is the book we all have been waiting for. It speaks to our struggles to understand our children and the nature of their God-given mission and is written with theological richness, practical insight, captivating and informative stories, and prophetic discernment. I cannot recommend this book enough.

Pastor Dr. Abera Habte
CEO and Founder, Elshaddai Television Network

Hope for the Second Generation is a masterpiece that reminds every immigrant family and host culture that God's calling is for generations. Dr. Tesema, a first-generation immigrant, intergenerational pastor, missiologist, and profound theologian presents his life experience working with second-generation immigrants. The writer's scholarly, biblical, cultural, sociological, and missiological presentation of the Missio Dei is thought-provoking, humbling, uplifting, and life-changing. It calls the second-generation to pursue something beyond the American Dream. Moreover, it applies to everyone as individuals, families, communities, churches, and nations— we too are called to rekindle Christianity through our callings and vocations. It is my prayer that every immigrant takes note and lives up to this higher calling and mission mandate.

Dr. Tilahun Mendedo
Former President, Concordia University, Alabama
Executive Development Officer, Lutheran Bible Translators

By tracing bi-cultural experiences and researching a biblical model of ministry in the Book of Acts, Dr. Tesema shows there is a hope for the second-generation diaspora. What makes Dr. Tesema's writing so vital, practical, and credible is that the man lives what he has written. *Hope for the Second Generation* is the work of a man who does help the second-generation diaspora to rekindle Christianity in the West. The book will help readers to grasp a new paradigm for ministering and equipping the second-generation diaspora.

Pastor Isaac H. Beraki
President, The Word of Truth Teaching Ministry
(Global Eritrean Ministry)

Hope for the Second Generation indeed contains the hope coveted for years in immigrant families. This work was birthed through the agony of a practical encounter that faced Pastor Tesfai and his family. It is not library research, though it incorporates the insights of scholars in the field. It is an answer to the cry: "How can we get a working solution?" Dr. Tesfai and his wife, Abeba, labored to seek an answer for this heart-burning and blood-boiling practical question. In the process of seeking a practical solution, they present suggestions to minimize the pain and confusion of the parents and children of the Diaspora community. This book is the first of its kind in Ethiopian & Eritrean Diaspora. Furthermore, it fulfills the mission of notifying the unsaved and edifying the saved by engaging the readers in this journey. Every parent who reads this work will say, "I was also there," and, "I wish I had known this before." I recommend this work for both immigrant parents and their children. I also recommend it for those who are in ministry and wrestle with the question, "What is the future of our children?" They will gain practical insights. May the good Lord bless you as you embark on this task of reading this work and, most importantly, raising and equipping the second generation.

Pastor Hailu Cherenet Biru, Ph.D.
Senior Pastor, Ethiopian Christian Fellowship
Los Angeles, California

At a time when *absolute truth* has been rejected and *relativism* has become the norm, many churches are earnestly praying for a revival to raise up a generation that seeks the face of God. Despite many efforts, however, my observation is that there is a general sense of despair on the subject. The good news is that God has answered our prayers in an unexpected way. A veteran pastor with many years of pastoral experience has written a book that is scholarly, well-versed, and pastorally and biblically balanced. I believe this book is a masterpiece for evangelicals rekindling our passion and opening our eyes to take equipping the second generation seriously.

Pastor Dr. Efrem Leakemariam
Ethiopian Evangelical Church
Toronto, Canada

This book helps to bridge the first and second generations' divide through profound Biblical insights. It explains how the first generation can leverage the potential powerful contribution of the second generation to build continuity and legacy. This is a must-read book for diaspora parents, church leaders, second-generation young people, and all who desire to see the Christian faith become strong in the Western hemisphere again.

Pastor Melkie Mebratu
Living Gospel Church
Winnipeg, Canada

Now is the perfect time for a book like this when the Church needs tools and resources to address and re-think its future. *Hope for the Second Generation* by Dr. Tesema comes out of 40 years of servant leadership and experience. I am a living testimony of his missional leadership and its impact, as I was raised and taught by most of the principles in the book. I am excited to see this come to light.

Reverend Muluneh Taye
Associate Pastor, Addis Kidan Lutheran Church
San Francisco, California

TABLE OF CONTENTS

FOREWORD

In late May 2017, I was privileged to lead a Bible study with a group of several Ethiopian leaders gathered in Washington D.C. They purposed to form an Ethiopian Mission Society aimed at reaching the Ethiopian populations growing in many urban centers in the United States, as well as sending missionaries to carry the saving Gospel of Jesus Christ to the Ethiopian Diaspora scattered throughout the world.

I focused my study on the theme of "the Diaspora" as St. Peter addressed it in his first general epistle: *Peter, an apostle of Jesus Christ, To those who are* **elect exiles of the Dispersion** *... according to the foreknowledge of God the Father, in the sanctification of the Spirit, for obedience to Jesus Christ and for sprinkling with his blood: May grace and peace be multiplied to you. (1 Peter 1:1–2).* I had spoken a number of times on this theme and even written briefly about it some years earlier[1], however, the audience was quite different this time.

These men and women self-identified as the Diaspora. It was more than a Biblical metaphor for our time, when Christians and their churches in America are systematically pushed from the centers of cultural influence to the periphery. It was even more than a powerful Biblical theme that runs from the early chapters of Genesis to the last page of Revelation. These brothers and sisters knew personally the pain and trauma of being uprooted from their homeland, their friends and families, their ancient culture and way of life, to be transplanted to a country that considers them foreigners, outsiders. They moved overnight from the centers of influence in their own nation and communities to the margins of minority status in America—culturally, socially, economically, and ethnically. Many were the losses of such dislocation; topping the list, however, was fear that they may lose their own children to a secular culture driven by radically different and potentially harmful values. No one understands these concerns better than Dr. Tesfai Tesema and his wife, Abeba.

I met Tesfai several years ago when I served as pastor at First Immanuel Lutheran Church, a multi-cultural congregation located in the heart of San Jose, CA. A mutual friend, Dr. Johannes Mengsteab, brought us together; our shared love of the Lord Jesus Christ and His heart for the world made us fast friends. I listened intently as Tesfai shared the story of his life—fleeing for his life from Ethiopia, coming to know the Lord Jesus through a Chinese national while working in Saudi Arabia, the persecution he and Abby endured on account of their witness for the Gospel, their church planting ministry in the Sudan, and finally their immigration to the United Sates and ministry among Ethiopians here. I believe you will be fascinated by his story as you read it in the coming pages.

In subsequent meetings Tesfai shared his burden for the 1.5 and 2.0 generation Ethiopian children living here in America. He deeply felt the struggles they were experiencing, pulled between the culture and values of their parents and the culture and values of their American peers. The children didn't fit exactly in either culture. They were in fact of a third culture; they were bi-cultural. They deeply appreciated the culture, including the Christian faith and values, of their parents. At the same time, their everyday lives revolved around an English-speaking world. English was becoming their first and perhaps only language. That created a number of challenges for the children's ability to stay connected to their Ethiopian roots, especially as regards their participation in the faith life of their parents. While remaining devout in their faith, they felt out of place in their parents' congregations, where all worship and social interaction took place in languages they barely understood. As their pastor, Tesfai devoted himself to finding a way to serve his traditionally Ethiopian congregation and, at the same time, his emerging group of English speaking, bi-cultural children. His pastoral burden moved him to enroll in the PhD in Missiology program at Concordia Theological Seminary in Ft. Wayne, IN. He immersed himself in the study of God's Word and missiological literature, especially that of cross-cultural and multi-cultural ministry. The result was a well-researched dissertation focused on the collective experience of 25 Ethiopian young people and their sojourn here in America. The book you have in your hands provides a popularized summary of Dr. Tesema's research. Behind the many invaluable facts and figures stand the personal stories of these children as they opened their hearts to share their real and often painful experiences. Their stories raise many questions that beg to be answered, especially by us Christians whom God has specifically called to "Love the sojourner."

While this book is a moving testimony to the struggles of 1.5 and 2.0 generation immigrant children in this country, it is not written primarily to look back on their experiences in sympathy but to look forward in the hope and faith anchored in God's Word and promises: *"Peter, an apostle of Jesus Christ, To those who are **elect exiles of the Dispersion** ... according to the foreknowledge of God the Father."*

That May morning in Washington D.C. I shared with the Ethiopian leaders that we can understand St. Peter's words in radically different ways depending upon our vantage point as we read them. The New International Version (NIV) of the Bible translates Peter's words from the vantage point that he is writing to encourage scattered and beleaguered Christians. The translation inserts a comma at the critical point—*"to God's elect, strangers in the world."* A comma stands between the words "elect" and "strangers," signaling the fact that being elect—chosen by God to be His children—is the essence of who we are. However, being strangers in this world and scattered all over it is *not*. These latter conditions are simply unfortunate circumstances that we must endure. The NIV does not stand alone in its use of a segregating "comma." The Authorized Version (KJV), Revised Standard Version (RSV), and New American Standard Bible (NASB)[2] all join in translating the Greek words that way.

What if, however, being an exile or sojourner scattered throughout the world was not an accident? What if it was the perfect, primary, and powerful will of our heavenly Father? The English Standard Version (ESV) translates this verse from this very different perspective. The ESV puts no comma to separate 'election' from 'being exiled' and by doing so changes everything. The absence of the comma tells us that God not only elected us to be His own but also chose us to be *strangers or exiles* in this world. Being strangers and being scattered across the globe are not unfortunate or tragic circumstances. They are conditions of God's deliberate choice, essential to His election and, therefore, to His divine purposes. St. Peter's letter was not primarily a letter expressing sympathy for the suffering the early Christians had to endure. Rather, it was a call to missionary action, a call not only to belong to God, but also to join God in His redeeming work for this broken world. In order to heed this call, Peter's readers needed to understand clearly and soberly who they were and what their divine purpose was in this world.

Pastor Tesfai carries the same hope in his heart for the 1.5 and 2.0 generation of Ethiopian immigrants of America that Peter carried in his for the Christian church of the First Century, that his own people would both understand their divine place and purpose in this world, and embrace it with all of their hearts, souls, minds, and strength. My prayer is that as you read this book the same divine hope and expectation that inspired Tesfai to write it will fill you!

Dr. Bob Newton
June 22, 2020

INTRODUCTION

This book really begins with a conversation between my wife, Abeba (Abby), and our eldest son, Abel. Abel was born in Khartoum, Sudan, during our two-year flight from Ethiopia, via Saudi Arabia and the Sudan, to North America. Although we brought him to the United States as a child, Abel's Amharic language skills were limited, and he refused to use the language in public. Abeba enrolled him and his younger brother, Daniel, in the Sunday School of an American church to supplement the spiritual education they were getting at the ethnic Ethiopian church I pastored in San Jose.

"Are you ready for church?" Abeba asked Abel that particular Sunday morning. "Which church?" Abel said. "Your church or my church?" She was horrified. "How can you say, 'your church'? Your father is the pastor!" "So what?" Abel said. "I don't understand what my father preaches. How can it be my church?" That's when it hit us. We were building a congregation of Ethiopians in America and we were happy. Unfortunately, our kids were not.

During this season of discovery, I met Pastor Bob Newton. He was pastoring a Lutheran church a few miles from ours, in downtown San Jose, California. I shared our challenge with him. Dr. Newton is an educator; he'd worked on the mission field in the Philippines for many years. "Your problem is cross-cultural," he said. "Right now, the church you pastor is one culture—Ethiopian. But your children are more American than they are Ethiopian. Consider developing a ministry that reaches across the culture gap, across the generation divide."

In response to Bob Newton's challenge, I enrolled in Concordia Theological Seminary (Fort Wayne, IN) in 2003, where I studied for three years, researching how to reach across the cultural divide to my own children. I tell the story of my work and discoveries in Section II of this book, 'Research.'

What is the problem? Together with my mentoring professor at Concordia, I worked to articulate it. We came up with this definition, which I would research and write my thesis on: *How do the Gen 1.5 and 2.0 immigrants from Ethiopia and Eritrea describe their identity? What are the implications of that for developing a culturally relevant ministry for them?* (I am including a Glossary at the back of this book to define terms like 'Gen 1.5 and 2.0.') Over the years I have found that the communication problem my wife and I had stumbled into is not unique to Ethiopian immigrants. Wherever I go and speak—and I've spoken with Africans from West Africa, like Ghanaians and Liberians, Hispanics from Colombia and South Korean immigrant parents—the first-generation immigrants to the U.S. often put their question this way: 'What's wrong with my children? They don't want to fit into our culture.' Bicultural children like Abel and Daniel actually have more in common with second-generation immigrant children from other countries such as Ghanaians, Nigerians, Koreans, Chinese, Hispanics etc. and white and black American children with whom they grew up than they do with a first-generation mother or pastor like Abeba and I.

What qualifies me to answer the question I'm posing? In Chapters 3–4 I tell my own story. I'm a first-generation Ethiopian. Abeba and I fled for our lives from our native Ethiopia and through many dangers, toils and snares, we arrived in the U.S.A. in 1984 as 'political refugees'. In 1989 I took the call to pastor an Ethiopian church planted two years earlier in San Jose, California, and we 'd probably still be there if the crisis in our family hadn't slapped us into action.

How to go about answering my question? For example, does the Bible have anything to say on this topic? Does the Bible speak about ministry across cultures? I detail my research in Chapters 5–7. In Chapter Five we look more closely at the 'Elect Sojourner.' In Bob Newton's excellent Foreword to this book, he describes the origin of this phrase in the Apostle Peter's first letter. The Elect Sojourner or Elect Exile is a character who appears throughout Scripture, starting with the nomad Abraham who left the sophisticated urban culture of Mesopotamia for a Bedouin life of wandering, herding sheep and living in tents, from ancient Syria to Egypt and back to Palestine. The Bible ends with the apostle John in exile on the Isle of Patmos. Acts Eight opens with the painful words 'Those who had been scattered preached the Word where they went' (Acts 8:4, NIV). I do a deep dive on the Greek phrase *'dia sporo,'* from which our English word Diaspora derives. Scattering is an experience from which people usually recoil. I'm sure you remember the horrific photos of Syrian refugees clinging to overflowing and fragile rubber rafts as they crossed the Mediterranean Sea to escape civil war. Or pictures of Salvadoran and Guatemalan mothers and fathers and children trekking northward in long lines, hoping to find asylum in the U.S. Ethiopians and Eritreans know 'scattering.' It was forced upon us by a Marxist tyrant. As distressing as it is, Bob Newton points out that 'scattering' is one of God's often used methods to advance his Kingdom.

How about cross-cultural ministry in the Bible? In Chapter 5 of this book, I examine the book of Acts account of how Jesus' commandment to 'Go ye therefore and teach all nations' resulted in His small band of believers multiplying to 3,000 bicultural and multilingual Jewish believers on Pentecost. Then I look at the Church in Antioch, where the leadership develops a deliberate strategy and selects leaders to reach out to another people group, the Greek Gentiles.

But we run into a dilemma. Recent church growth strategy in the U.S., articulated forcefully by church leaders like Donald McGavran and Peter Wagner, state the Homogeneous Unit Principle (HUP)—the importance of cultural similarity among members for churches to grow. As Wagner put it: "Try not to allow diverse social and cultural elements to mix on the congregational level any more than necessary. Churches must be built as much as possible within homogeneous units if they are to maintain a sense of community among believers."[3] McGavran and Wagner inspired a whole generation of church planters with the idea that in order to grow and thrive, a church should be made up of people who are culturally like each other.

If I wanted to advise young church planters in our Ethiopian community, I was going to have to deal with HUP, the Homogeneous Unit Principle. In fact, as I wrote earlier, Abel and Daniel share more cultural experience with second-generation kids of other ethnicities than they do with a first-generation Ethiopian. They've attended the same elementary and high schools, speak the same English language and its slang, dance to the same music and watch the same movies, they share the same bicultural personality as these other bicultural children of immigrants, regardless of where in the world their Old Country was located. Does this resemblance to other bicultural children make them into a homogeneous unified group? Does their story in fact prove the HUP?

Chapter 7 relates the story of my research. To understand the bicultural soul of the children of the immigrant generation, I sought out twenty-five young Ethiopians and Eritreans. With the help of my dissertation advisors, my professors, I developed a list of questions that would probe the soul of the bicultural person. It took me two years of phone calls and in-person meetings to do the interviews and my son, Daniel, transcribed their recorded statements into 500 single-spaced pages of text. I include several actual stories to give you a flavor of the interviews. In Chapters 1 and 2 of this book, interviewees Rahel and Girmachew speak frankly about growing up second-generation in America. I discovered six themes among the interviewees, which I labelled: Ethiopian-ness, Fitting In, Blackness, American-ness, In-Between and In-Both and Spirituality. Go to the Glossary at the back to see my definitions of these terms. Here are a couple of my findings: A number of the interviewees said, 'I am too American to be Ethiopian ... I will say I am Ethiopian-American; Ethiopian by heritage and American by culture and nation.' Most of the interviewees said they had experienced some form of discrimination, sometimes race discrimination from peers, sometimes discrimination from their parents' generation because they didn't fit into Ethiopian culture. Most relevant for my thesis, the interviewees described their religious experience. A young man who is highly committed in an American church said, 'I left the Ethiopian church because of cultural barriers. There was no benefit there for me since I hardly speak the language. Most people of my generation feel the same way. Those who were born in Ethiopia and have Amharic language skills stay. Most people who attend the Ethiopian church in America attend for cultural reasons.'

My research led me to a key finding which I report in the Conclusion (Chapter 13). *The children of the immigrants need their own church, where they will speak English and fellowship with other biculturals, including non-Ethiopians.*

I emerged from seminary fired up to plant churches just like that and I spent four years in San Jose, launching church plants for second-generation Ethiopians, like my sons. None of these efforts resulted in a church that lived. But through this process, which I report in Chapter Eight, I discovered God had a better role for me. I would not be the church planter for this demographic group but the equipper of young people who would do the plant. I report how I again found a Biblical model, this time in the tale of Mordecai and Esther from the book of Esther. As the child of exiled Jewish immigrants in the strange new world of Persia, Esther depended on her uncle, Mordecai, the First-Generation immigrant. He saw the advantage she had as a bicultural Jew and Persian, encouraged her to enter the national beauty contest and after she won and became queen, he advised her. I see myself today as a Mordecai, building a bridge between the generation of the children, who desperately feel the need for their own ministry, and their parents' generation, who hold the authority, power and finances to disregard and roadblock the children or encourage and support them.

In Chapters 9, 10, and 11, I recount real-life church planting experiments. I 'play Mordecai' and work with young leaders who attempt to launch ministries in Washington, DC (Silver Spring, MD), London (U.K.), Toronto and Minneapolis/St. Paul. The results vary. I think you'll find their stories fascinating.

Then, just as I was finishing this book, America fell apart. Covid-19 stunned the country and left us locked down in our homes. And a white policeman knelt on black George Floyd's neck in Minneapolis and murdered him and protests filled the streets of our major cities. My friend, Bob Newton, again asked the probing question. As we all recoiled from the social and racial chaos, Dr. Bob sent me an email. "Is this a Kairos moment?" he asked. "A fullness-of-time moment for hearing the gospel. America needs voices that go beyond 'should we tear down this statue or that one'? These are band-aid solutions on a country that needs to be healed from the inside out. Ethiopian-Americans may have a unique position because they too have dark skins and have suffered because of it. And they are Christians. What do they have to tell us?'

I reached out again to my circle of second-generation leaders, especially the ones who had planted churches. 'The Editor of *Christianity Today* writes that the Church in America has not taken the sin of racism with the gravity and seriousness it deserves. Do you agree that churches intentionally preach spiritual salvation but neglect to preach justice? How are you and your church processing the murder of George Floyd—the event, Black Lives Matter demonstrations, and the lootings?' Several young pastors responded. I am including Chapter 12, my interviews with Ebenezer, the 29-year-old pastor of Perazim Church in Minneapolis, Ground Zero for these events. Pastor Ebenezer tells about a worship service he conducted on the hill overlooking the Floyd Memorial site on June 15 of this year. He also recounts his own journey from not caring about such things to deep distress when he saw the George Floyd video. He sees a parallel in his life with Queen Esther, who moves from indifference 'because of her privilege' to passionate engagement with the fate of the Jews.

Finally, I wrap it all up with a 2500-word Conclusion and action plan for those scattered immigrants who want to launch a 'culturally relevant gospel ministry for the next generation.' Jesus told Peter, 'I will build my church, and the gates of Hades will not prevail against it' (NIV). We know that's His plan and we can be confident He will succeed. Could it be, as Pastor Ebenezer asks, that if his generation rests in its privilege and does not 'lean in,' that God will replace them, as Mordecai warned Esther? Could it be that he and his colleagues in Minneapolis and all second-generation believers were born for such a time as this?

Tesfai Tesema
September 1, 2020
San Francisco, California

PART ONE

Stories

ONE

Rahel and the Ethiopian Path She Didn't Take

"There is an ideal Ethiopian path," Rahel says. "It's linked with Ethiopian culture, and it doesn't matter whether you are evangelical Christian, like we were, or Ethiopian Orthodox, or even Ethiopian Muslim—I see the pattern in all of them. You go straight out of high school to college; you graduate; you get married; you have children; you buy a house. If you don't take that path people say: 'You've been Americanized too long.'

"I didn't take the path."

Rahel's parents moved from Ethiopia, by way of several years in Norway, to Columbus, Ohio, when she was four. Her father was a pastor and he launched an outreach to the Ethiopian immigrant community in Columbus. Her parents tell her she spoke both Norwegian and Amharic when they arrived in Columbus and in order to fit in, she pretended to talk gibberish English. Once she nailed English a year later, she was accent-free.

For Pastor D and his wife, like many immigrant parents, the freewheeling Nineteen Eighties America delivered an enormous shock to their sense of right and wrong. They tried to shield their two daughters. The girls understood the family rules, even though they were mostly unspoken. *'You will not talk to boys.' 'You will not hang out.' 'You will not go out to parties or clubs.' 'You will not drink or do drugs.'* The family attended church together every Sunday and when the church put on a weekend conference, the whole family attended from Friday night through Sunday night.

"Up until I turned fifteen, I was very active in my parents' church. I got baptized and filled with the Holy Spirit and I was headed down the ideal Ethiopian path. Then I began to wonder: Am I missing something? I didn't know what it was. Just a feeling that my parents had sheltered me from experiencing the world. My friends in high school drank and partied. I didn't do that. But I remember thinking: 'I've got to see what the world has to offer.' In high school, she begged for her own separate phone line to connect freely with her friends. When the parents went to bed, she and her young sister, Hellen, opened their bedroom window and snuck out.

"At age twenty-one I became pregnant. I was extremely scared. I remember morning sickness and opening up the spigot to run the water so my parents couldn't hear me puking. They kept asking and I lied and said, No, I'm NOT pregnant. People talked, because in our culture you waited till you were married. People didn't say: Is Rahel pregnant? They said: Pastor's daughter is pregnant. I couldn't work up the courage to sit down and tell my parents the truth. They only knew for sure the day my son arrived.

"It was very difficult for my parents. They came to the hospital for the birth, and they said Whatever you need, we will do. I felt grateful. Of course, they fell in love with Jim right away."

Rahel describes her relationship with her son's father as 'dysfunctional.' She became desperate. Meanwhile, in 2002, her parents moved from Ohio to a suburb of Washington, DC, where her father took a new pastorate. "I continued as a single parent in the city of Columbus. His father still lives there, and Jim had a wonderful relationship with his dad, but things weren't working out for me." When someone offered her a one-way ticket to DC a year later, Rahel grasped it. She took Jim along and says she breathed an enormous sigh of relief when the plane touched down in DC. She plugged into her parents' church, rededicated her life to Christ and began a new life living at her parents' house. She worked minimum wage jobs to finance her life with Jim and the schooling she needed to get credentialed for a career.

"I was thirty and I went back to school full-time."

She put in eighteen-hour days and pumped herself up with Five Hour Energy drinks to stay awake until two or three every morning while she studied. She had determined to win certification as a nurse and she wondered, many days: "Can I reach that goal? But I was gonna do what I had to do in order to do what I wanted to do." She was considering Emergency Room Trauma care because she loved the adrenaline rush that came with emergencies—accidents, gunshot wounds, life-or-death situations. She also encountered substance abuse cases in the county jail where she worked. Initially, she felt no interest in addiction work.

She says her interest level changed as she witnessed drug abuse in the suburbs of the nation's capital rise to epidemic proportions. Today she is employed at an outpatient substance abuse clinic, working with people who struggle with addiction to drugs and alcohol and, frequently, mental health issues like depression, suicide and personality disorders. Even though she had never had a problem with drug abuse, she found she identified with her clients' bad choices, with their depression, with their desire to fill an emotional void with something powerful. The patients would ask her: why do you do what you do? You seem happy, why is that? Reborn in her commitment to Christ, she would occasionally share Christ as the answer to their problems.

"I feel called to my job as a substance abuse nurse. I'll do it till the day I can't do it anymore!"

Rahel's parents helped with Tim and made great personal time sacrifices for the boy. Although Rahel and Jim's father continued to care for their son, her parents regularly looked after him. Without their help, she says, raising him alone would have been difficult. At thirteen, Jim asked to return to Ohio to live with his dad. During his three years in Ohio, he did not participate in Christian fellowship because his dad wasn't a churchgoer, but when he returned to his mother at sixteen, Jim plugged into the new young adult service that Rahel's younger sister, Hellen, and her husband, Steve, had launched.

Twenty years after she went out looking for what was missing, Rahel still wrestles with 'the Ethiopian path' as she talks with her son about his future. "I grew up with a mom and dad. I was raised to believe there is a pattern, which I didn't follow. I tell my son: you know, Jim, the way I did things wasn't the proper order. I'm very happy that you're here. But I don't want you to repeat what I did. I want something better for you." She confesses that she can't really identify with her son's life. There is a gap between the way she was raised and what her son is living out. What worked, when her parents raised her, does not feel like the right approach for raising a son today.

"In my culture, growing up, if you were to say: 'Mom, I have a boyfriend,' you might hear: 'What do you mean, a boyfriend? Why do you need him?'" A better response today, she believes, might be a question: 'Why do you feel the need to have a boyfriend right now?' "Our culture pushes kids away when we say: 'Don't talk to me about that. Don't bring it up. I don't want to hear it.' What happens is the child will find what he wants to know from an outsider, and it may include harmful information. That's what I'm learning from my son. If he has a question we will sit down right there and have a conversation from a Biblical perspective. I'm not going to say: Why are you asking me this? *We're going to have a conversation.*"

At eighteen, Jim owns a car, gifted to him by his father, and plays high school football, both life assets that expose him to multiple temptations. Rahel is talking about college with him, and he says he doesn't want to go to school and pile up fifty or sixty thousand dollars of debt in exchange for a degree he may never use. "I'm 100% with you," Rahel says, and they agree he will go to community college. She says comments from some in the Ethiopian-American community trouble her. "They don't care how much debt it takes. They just want the child to get the degree so they can say: My child graduated from XYZ University." In her job she meets substance abusers who say a father or mother abused them, pushing the child, living out through the child the doctor or lawyer career they were never able to personally accomplish. She sees children who feel overwhelmed by pressure from parents to succeed.

She doesn't blame her parents for her not taking the Ethiopian path. "I appreciate them and the sacrifices and struggles they made for me. I wasn't the easiest teenager. I try to convince them today: You might feel you didn't do as much as you could have but I know you did the best. Not just the best you could but *the best*. I'm here because of your prayers. Whatever path I chose is not a reflection on you."

In 2020, Hellen and brother-in-law, Steve, will launch a new church in the DC area. Rahel joined the core team, and they are training for the church launch. What does 'core team member' mean? Ministry opportunities abound, she says. For starters, she will work with the greeters ministry, and 'make sure every visitor gets greeted with a smile and acknowledged by name. Even if they never return, they've been acknowledged and that's important.' But she and her sister dream of launching a substance abuse ministry at the new church. Hellen also grew up with the sense she was missing something. Although Rahel didn't know of it until much later, Hellen filled the void she felt with cocaine, an addiction she continued for eleven years until she was miraculously delivered. "So, this is a passion we share. She brings her experience; I bring my training."

Because she loved Amharic worship songs and understood the gist of the Amharic preaching, Rahel joined her father's church when she first moved to DC. But today she prefers English language worship and preaching. One important reason for that is Jim—English worship brings her and Jim together.

Is she still Ethiopian? Rahel laughs but she gets very excited about this question. "I actually don't like it when other Ethiopians tell me I'm Americanized, just because I was raised here. My veins still bleed Ethiopian. I was born there! I love Ethiopian culture—I love our hospitality; I love how family-oriented we are. I just love the love."

She has a plan to return to Ethiopia for the first time since her early childhood, as soon as her son establishes himself in college. No, she has no memories of Ethiopia. "It's going to be brand spanking new for me." Her uncles and aunts still live in Ethiopia, along with cousins she doesn't remember. She worries whether she will be able to take a decent shower there because she's heard hot showers are not easily available. But perhaps there will be bigger challenges on the trip. Her Amharic language is still solid, but what about the people she meets and how they think? Will they perceive her to be Ethiopian or American?

"I hope to break my stereotypes. I hope I experience in Ethiopia what I experienced growing up Ethiopian-American, which is the love and the Oneness of our community. I'm going home!"

Girmachew, the Ethiopian Fiddler on the Roof

"It's a beautiful name," Girmachew says. "But not here in the States. In high school kids nicknamed me 'Pikachu' or 'Garbanzo Beans.' I changed my name from Girmachew to Girma so my dental patients could pronounce it. The little kids call me 'Dr. Grandma' and I correct their pronunciation. So, when our twins were born, we decided on names that wouldn't make life difficult, growing up here in the States. We called them Maya and Grace. 'Maya,' in Amharic, means a lens you look through. So, you see the balance—we haven't completely left Ethiopian culture with 'Maya'—she was born first—and we're solidly American with 'Grace.' That's just who we are."

Like the Jewish fiddler on the roof, Girmachew finds himself on the rooftop, balancing between two cultures. After twenty-three years, he believes he's achieved a pretty good balance.

His parents brought Girmachew and his siblings to San Jose, California, in 1996. He was eleven. "I was just in awe of America," he recalls. "Coming from a Third World Country, it was like drinking water out of a fire hose, trying to swallow a culture I'd never seen before." His parents enrolled him in the sixth grade of the local public school. He could barely speak English. His class was watching the movie *Roots*, Alex Haley's famous story of Black America, the story of black men and women transported in leg-irons on slave ships from Africa to work in the cotton fields of white American plantation owners in the pre-Civil War South. "We didn't have a history of slavery in Ethiopia and watching it was very, very difficult for me. Especially the questions the kids asked afterward."

They asked him what life was like in Africa. Most of them had only seen TV portrayals of the famines and jungles of Africa. 'Did you have a lion for a pet?' someone asked. Someone else asked, 'How did you get here? By boat?' They didn't know Ethiopia had airplanes! How should one respond to such ignorance? 'I swam,' he told the questioner. And No, Ethiopia had no history of slavery or race discrimination of the American variety.

Ethiopia had other assets that he only realized as time passed. "The other day at the clinic we were talking. My American colleagues told me what they did as kids—lots of video games—and how they take their kids on field trips now to show them some real life. What? They said to me. You didn't play *that* video game when you were a kid? You didn't take a field trip with your school a couple times a year? And I said: No, in Ethiopia every day was a field day!"

Growing up thirty years ago in Addis Ababa, the Ethiopian capital, was different than childhood in an American city. Electricity was optional, for one thing. Some days it came on, some days it stayed off. "We didn't bug our parents to buy toys at the store. We made toys." He and his friends constructed soccer balls from milk containers and used wire hangers to chase the balls along the road. They played marbles in the mud. They hooked rubber hoses together to make tires for their toy wagons. "It was completely and utterly fun," Girmachew recalls.

"But in San Jose, as an eleven-year-old, I was walking into stores filled with toys. That's unfortunate! The toy is already made for you. It takes your imagination out of the picture."

None of those memories, however, made him question his parents' decision to leave Ethiopia for the U.S. "I had to respect them. I didn't talk back, and education was Number One." In addition, people back in Ethiopia had described the States as the destination of a lifetime. Even as a befuddled eleven-year-old, Girmachew understood: this was a wide-open land where he could thrive.

First, however, he needed to conquer junior high school. He was a swimmer tossed overboard into a vast and perilous ocean. Language was the first shark he encountered. He was slotted into an ESL (English as Second Language) class with Hispanic and Indian immigrant kids. The English words that he did know needed to be reshaped to be understood, because the British English accent taught in East African schools didn't make sense to listeners here. The slang words used by his American classmates seemed like complete gibberish. Familiar phrases, like 'that's bad,' meant 'that's good'! Initially he did not join any group of students, although he sat with other immigrant kids who were all suffering the same obstacles. Eventually, other Ethiopian immigrant schoolmates found him, and they clustered together. "If it wasn't for them, I would have drowned completely."

Girmachew's parents were each working two jobs, paid at minimum wage, to cover the costs of housing and food. "They couldn't understand what I was experiencing. In fact, I was absorbing the culture much faster than they were because the younger you are when you come, the bigger the pores are in your sponge. I was figuring out American culture on my own, looking at it through the lenses of my twelve and thirteen-year-old peers."

Three years into America, Girmachew entered the public high school. At the high school, he found far fewer immigrant kids and far more African-American youths from the community. "I wanted to join African-American culture because they were the most welcoming. They were also the coolest group." The hip-hop and rhythm-and-blues music culture was ubiquitous. African-American kids wore head sets and listened to rap music. Boys wore baggy pants and sagged them down their backsides. "I started braiding my hair when I entered my junior year." His parents didn't understand. Television shows and news presented such behavior as fringe, the trappings of a failed thug culture.

"My parents wanted us to look like white collar professionals because that's what they wanted us to be." Fortunately, his three-year-older brother Joseph was already paving the trail, braiding his hair, wearing baggy clothes, but then moving on to college. His parents softened their criticism. "So, what if I wore baggy pants if I was getting straight A's?"

Looking back, Girmachew agrees he has experienced prejudice throughout his American experience. "In junior high, just the fact that I didn't understand the culture, that I had a weird name and a strong accent led to discrimination. But the group that held their arms wide open to me was the African-Americans, unlike the group who turned their backs on me in high school, the Caucasian kids. I can only attribute the difference to my skin color."

He experienced a lot of discrimination in college, which continued into dental school.

"In dental school, one of the really good professors took me aside. He was African-American. He told me the way to win is to get your degree. Get the same degree they do and then you will stand on the same platform they do. Fight then, if you like, but don't do it now. *The Denver Post* did an investigative report on my dental school because there had been complaints of discrimination from the African-Americans students at this predominantly Caucasian school. *The Post* asked to interview me. I told them: Look, I'm here to get a degree. I'm having a great experience. If someone wants to give me a hard time, I mainly overlook it. If you want me to study twice as hard, I'll do it. I'm going to give you the benefit of the doubt until you try to come between me and my success and then I'll either go through you or around you."

After dental school, Girmachew experienced discrimination again when he applied for a job. He and his white fellow graduates were all applying to well-known dental clinics. They were getting multiple interviews. He was getting none. He called the recruiter of the dental clinic where he really wanted to work. 'My colleagues are getting interviews with you and I'm still waiting,' he told the recruiter. 'Why?' The recruiter said: 'You know, we don't hire international students.' 'I'm not an international student,' Girmachew said. 'I've lived in the States twenty years and I'm a U.S. citizen.' The recruiter apologized for misunderstanding, based purely on his name. "That's when I knew the plus and minus power of a name. 'Girmachew' just sounds foreign."

Clutching his diploma from dental school, Girmachew was poised for life in his adopted hometown, Denver. Step Two: marriage. Twelve years earlier he had responded to Dr. Tesema's question about his ideal for his wife: Given a choice between marriage to someone who was Ethiopian, but not a 'born-again Christian' and marriage to a woman who was Caucasian and a believer, which would he choose? He responded that he would choose the Caucasian because he believed his faith in Christ was more important than his identity as an Ethiopian. But preference-wise, he still preferred an Ethiopian, or better yet, an Ethiopian American like himself. He had dated newly arrived Ethiopian women, dated Caucasians, dated African-Americans. "I found I could get along with pretty much any culture. But my preference? An Ethiopian-American, someone who had lived in the States longer than she had lived in Ethiopia."

A very good Ethiopian friend wanted to set him up on a blind date with a woman he knew in Minnesota. "My first question wasn't: Is she Ethiopian? It was: Is she a believer? If so, tell me more about her relationship with Christ. A relationship between someone in Minnesota and me in Colorado didn't sound workable to me but I promised my friend I would give her a call. If nothing else, perhaps I could make a friend. He didn't tell me upfront that she was his cousin, an Ethiopian.

"On the first call, I just clicked with Tsion. Her passion for Christ put her into a special light for me. She spoke Amharic. She also spoke English pretty well. 'O my God, she gets me! And I get her!' We clicked all over the place." A little over a year, Girmachew married Tsion.

Girmachew elaborates on the role his Christian faith has played in making him the man he is today. "I got saved in San Jose when I was thirteen or fourteen. The youth group in my parents' church caravanned to a conference in Los Angeles. I had an encounter with God I will never forget. Just unspeakable joy that resonates within me to this day. It's the comfort place I go to regardless of what I'm experiencing in life."

As he remembers his high school days, he was continually trying to fit into identities that didn't work. "Once I found my identity in Christ, it got easier to relate to a specific group because I could be myself." Girmachew's family moved to Denver when he was sixteen. "The youth group at the evangelical church we attended in Denver was mostly Ethiopian-Americans. I made friends and they helped me secure my identity in Christ. To this day my closest friends are friends I made in that youth group."

Sometime in high school he began to realize the value of his multiple identities as Ethiopian, American and Christian. "I could bridge the two cultures. An Ethiopian-American born here in the States would come up to me and say: My mom bothers me. She doesn't understand why I have a lot of female friends. I told him: I have the same problem you do. My mom says the same thing to me. Our culture is not like the Ethiopian culture they grew up in. They don't get why us teens like to wrestle and hang out until midnight. Then I would turn around and tell his parents: Hey, it's okay. I know he's doing this; he's doing that. That's actually not bad behavior in this culture. He's normal! Because I spent eleven years in Ethiopia, I understood both sides."

But deep down, Girmachew's soul was Ethiopian. His friend David, once a child immigrant from Ethiopia like Girmachew, launched the Avenue Church, a spin-off of an Ethiopian church but "run completely by our generation, Ethiopian-Americans. The pastor, the usher, the worship leaders were all Ethiopian-Americans and everything was in English. I thought right from the start: Wow! I belong here!"

He'd discovered something about himself back in San Jose. At the Ethiopian church he had joined as a new believer, the youth pastor conducted the Bible studies in Amharic. He began to read the Bible in Amharic. Reading passages was tedious and slow and when he finished a passage, he often had to reread in order to understand what he had read the first time. "I gave up," he says. "After all, my goal wasn't to cling to the Amharic language. My goal was to understand God. I switched to the English Bible. When I read a passage in English, the first time through I understood it. My spiritual life began to grow like crazy."

The Avenue Church experience, wonderful as it was, didn't last long. After founding the church, David left his post as pastor. Disillusioned, Girmachew didn't want to attend any longer and he left. "Currently I go to an Ethiopian Evangelical Church. I honestly love worshipping in Amharic. But when it comes to the teaching of the Word of God, I prefer American style preaching. Someone like T.D. Jakes or John Lanier. I have only stuck with the Ethiopian church to help out with the youth group."

His wife, Tsion, prefers the Ethiopian congregation and he stays because he believes it's important for them to go to church together. "But these days I can't invite a lot of my friends to the church because they don't speak Amharic. That's harsh. I also don't expect my girls to enjoy Ethiopian church after a certain point, either. Today they're babies but they're going to grow up more American than Ethiopian. After they come back from college, what are the odds they'll come to Ethiopian church? I'd say 10%. That's being generous. It's probably more like 5%."

Twenty years after his family emigrated to the States, Girmachew fulfilled a longtime dream and took a trip to Ethiopia.

He only had a few memories left of Ethiopia—memories of himself as a kid, of his old neighborhood, of the drive from home to school. Ethiopia hit him like an ice-cold shower, the same level of shock he had felt when he first came to the States. In Addis Ababa, cranes and bulldozers were noisily lifting girders, scooping rubble all over the city. Buildings he remembered had been demolished. "Everywhere I encountered noise and traffic and pollution and dust. It must have been the same when I was a kid, but I didn't notice it back then. Now it plugged up my nose and eyes. I pushed past the annoyance, thinking: When I open my mouth, they'll realize I'm one of them and they'll exclaim 'you're still like us!' But it didn't happen that way. I felt different. They looked me over like I was an alien. We spoke the same language but carrying on a conversation felt strange. We Americans were loud. I talked louder than my boyhood chums and they seemed very timid to me. We Americans seemed bigger.

"I realized then how my years in the U.S. had morphed me. I could not say I was fully Ethiopian. I had also *never* felt fully American. Can I be both Ethiopian and American? I enjoyed that trip, but could I live in Ethiopia again? I could not. Going forward, my life was going to be in the U.S. Yes, I was Ethiopian-American.

THREE

Tesfai's Unlikely Story

The 1970s were a traumatic time for my family and for Ethiopia. It was a time of drought, civil unrest, and cancelled schools. People, especially the students, challenged the government of Haile Selassie Emperor of Ethiopia. In 1974 the military joined them and overthrew the Emperor and imprisoned him. I was in my early twenties, just out of high school.

I listened to the philosophy of the new Derg military government. They told us appealing things about Marxist communism. Everyone was going to be equal. Like many young Ethiopians, I had come to see that our country's feudal society—where fewer than 10% of the people controlled the majority of the land—was unjust and needed to be overturned. My own parents owned land and lived comfortably but I believed the new Marxist rulers who promised to bring equality between the rich and the poor by creating a system ruled by the peasants and the working class. I joined the new government as a leader in helping nomads leave their nomadic lifestyle and become farmers on collective farms, according to the model of socialist ideals.

Many of the students who initiated the initial unrest grew unhappy that the military had co-opted their movement. They organized an underground party called the EPRP— the Ethiopian People's Revolutionary Party. Although I was working for the government, I also secretly joined the EPRP. Things were peaceful until the Derg decided to consolidate power and the EPRP tried unsuccessfully to remove the Derg and take power. The Derg responded with the Red Terror. Over the next two years they killed thousands of Ethiopians, including my younger brother, who was also an EPRP member. Sadly, I and many young Ethiopians who believed the Marxist philosophy and sacrificed tremendously to bring about change found it was mostly false promises. But right then, I still believed.

I was arrested but then released because the arresting authorities didn't uncover my EPRP connection. I knew I had to leave Ethiopia before I was discovered. Airports and exit visas were impossible. I decided to escape on foot, avoiding the railways and main roads. The safest route ran across the Danakil Depression—one of the hottest, cruelest deserts on earth, to reach the border with Djibouti, our mostly Muslim neighbor country on the Red Sea. The border was 130 miles away. I believe I succeeded only because of the prayers of my mother and father. In Djibouti I became a homeless refugee, living on the streets but again, my mother back in Ethiopia interceded. She contacted a relative, who held a job and an apartment in Jeddah, Saudi Arabia. This relative came to Djibouti looking for me and he brought me a one-month tourist visa to Saudi and his promise that he could get me a job there.

In hindsight, I see God was ordering my steps. Shortly after I landed in Jeddah, our relative went back to Djibouti and the new U.S. refugee program relocated him to the U.S. I was stuck in his apartment in Jeddah, jobless. Even that was a good thing. If I had relocated to the U.S. with him then, I would never have found Jesus. Or my wife Abby.

Friends of our relative helped me find a job with a Singaporean construction company. The job was building a huge mansion for a wealthy Jeddah banker, in a compound outside of Jeddah City, surrounded by a fence. The remote location was fortunate because the immigration officers didn't come looking for me after my tourist visa expired. On my third day on the job, I met Khou, a mechanical engineer who worked for the company. 'What religion are you?" He asked. It was a common question in a country like Saudi Arabia where people practice their religion publicly as Muslims. I said I was a Christian. In fact, as a convinced Marxist, I didn't believe in God. My family was Christian—that was true. But my childhood experience in the Orthodox Ethiopian Church had been meaningless. The Orthodox used a centuries-old liturgy in their worship—Ge'ez, an ancient, no longer spoken Ethiopian language which the church used like the Roman Catholics use Latin. On Christian holidays the adults asked us children to kiss the Bible. Not read or understand it. Still, since my family was Christian, that meant I was too, didn't it?

Khou was happy to meet another 'Christian.' He invited me to his weekly Bible study. What? An educated young man who studies the Bible? In my experience, people who followed Jesus were backward, uneducated people. But Khou was a very smart mechanical engineer. He sounded interesting!

The Bible study upset me. On the first night, Khou and his friend were studying Second Timothy 3. In that passage, the Apostle Paul says in the End Times people will become lovers of themselves, lovers of money, proud, boastful, selfish, disobedient to their parents, appearing godly but not really so. I was filled with terror. I did remember one thing about God from my Orthodox childhood. God judges sinners. This Bible passage made it clear I was a sinner. I had escaped the Derg communists only to fall under the unseen fist of a supernatural judge. He had found me, and he would certainly kill me. Of course, Khou and his friend had no idea I was thinking these thoughts. They gave me the New Testament to take home. Back home, I tried to locate the passage again, but I couldn't find it, so I had no choice but to start reading at the beginning of the book and that's where I found the picture of Billy Graham. Beneath his photo there was a sketch of a great chasm with a man figure on the left and a triangle representing God on the other side and the Sinner's Prayer in black and white as the way to cross the chasm to reach God. I knew exactly what I needed to do. At 8:30pm that same night I got down on my knees and prayed that prayer.

That's how Jesus found this terrified refugee in Saudi Arabia.

A few months later, on a visit to friends in Jeddah, I met an Eritrean man. He asked about the New Testament he saw sticking out of my breast pocket. Are you a Christian? He asked. This time I could truthfully say I was! He invited me to the Eritrean Bible group that met on Friday mornings. I met Abeba Gilabzi there and we fell in love. We married privately because Saudi law does not recognize Christian marriage. Some people who worked at the U.S. Embassy gave us Christian tracts and videos in Arabic that we could share with our Arab friends. My wife Abeba (Abby), her friends and the rest of our church group, began witnessing to immigrant Ethiopians and to Saudis. One of the women Abby witnessed to betrayed her to the Saudi police. Although Abby and her friend were both five months pregnant, the Saudis locked them up in prison on a charge of blasphemy. Saudi law says you can preach and pray with other Christians but doing so with Saudi Muslims, the vast majority of the country, will trigger severe penalties on you. After one month in prison, the Saudis deported Abby and her friend, together with us husbands, to Sudan.

Again, God's hand was moving. Because of the civil war between Ethiopia and the breakaway province of Eritrea, five hundred thousand Ethiopians had jammed into the Sudan as refugees. In Khartoum, the Sudanese capital, a church that held services in Tigrinya, the language of Eritrea, existed. However, there were no churches in Amharic, our Ethiopian national language. So, two other couples and I began meetings in Amharic under a huge tree in the middle of a really nice garden at the Sudan Interior Mission. I preached and taught the Bible and prayed with the refugees. God brought people who were desperate for his touch. A visitation, God's revival, broke out among the refugees! Right from the start we experienced miracles of healing and deliverance from demons. Many Ethiopians—hundreds upon hundreds of them—came to faith in Jesus. It was after one of those healings that I first began to wonder: Could God be calling me to be a pastor?

The U.S. Consul General in Jeddah applied for U.S. visas for us, in accordance with President Reagan's new sympathy for people who became refugees because of their religious faith. In March 1984, Abby, Baby Abel, Abby's under age brother Efrem, and I flew together to the U.S. First Methodist Church Fellowship of Chevy Chase, Maryland, sponsored us, took care of us financially and found us a two bedroom in nearby Silver Spring.

We were comfortable, we were safe at last. But after a few months I grew restless again. What were we here for? In the Sudan we had witnessed the Gospel *in power*. People were healed, lives changed, the church grew and planted daughter churches. I'd been sharing the gospel every day. Should I become a pastor now in the States? I wouldn't use words like 'I felt called to the ministry' to describe what was going on inside. I didn't know this way of speaking but the feelings were there. I had felt this way from the night I committed my life to Christ in Saudi Arabia—I wanted to share the Good News with seekers.

I'd have to get training. But for at purpose? For what church? For what people? I could never return to Ethiopia where the Derg Government was still looking for me. Returning to Sudan as a refugee didn't seem like an option either. In Jeddah we had heard about the Rhema Bible Training Center in Tulsa, Oklahoma and seen their monthly magazine. From Maryland, I wrote to Rhema and next thing we were on our way to Oklahoma. Like Abraham, we told each other, going out for what purpose and what goal we couldn't guess but we knew one thing. God said: Go!

For two years I trained at Rhema, and Abby trained there too, for a year. Daniel, our second son, was born in Oklahoma and I began to think about how to get into full-time ministry. We heard about Ethiopian churches starting up in several large American cities and their pastors invited me to preach. Every other weekend I was flying to Dallas, where my good friend, Pastor Zeleke, was planting a church for Ethiopian refugees. Southwest Airlines had a deal, a weekend fare of nineteen dollars! Zeleke's church had only thirty members, but I got to help church plant and meet Ethiopian pastors who were planting churches in Atlanta, Washington, DC, Chicago and San Jose! I met Pastor Seifu, the pastor in San Jose and then something amazing happened. Pastor Zeleke decided to move to Denver to do a new church plant, while Seifu would replace him in Dallas. Did I want to come and take over the San Jose Church? Yes, I did!

The Ethiopian community in San Jose was almost

all singles. These people who had fled for their lives from Ethiopia couldn't return to Ethiopia to find a mate because the Derg was ruling, so they chose mates from our group or from other American cities and I married off a lot of singles. In the beginning, we had twenty some people, and then an immigrant flood began. What caused the flood? Family visas, marriages and then the U.S. government Diversity Visa Program, which favored people from a few countries, including Ethiopia as one of a select group of African countries. I was the sole pastor of our church, and I did everything—preach, administrate, *everything*. That's a difference about immigrant churches. They are not only places of worship; they are literally the only family a refugee might have in the U.S. The pastor is the older brother, the uncle. People look to him for everything social. It's not just a Sunday thing. People treated me, in fact, like a father. We stayed fourteen years.

I probably would have stayed with this church forever if it hadn't been for the crisis developing in our church and in our home. We were not prepared for what our children would need, in terms of church and relationships. Our kids preferred to speak English and Abeba and I were fine with that. But deeper gaps were opening between us and our kids because of culture and language. In American churches, the leadership provided Sunday School for the children. Those of us who came to Protestant Christian faith out of the Ethiopian Orthodox church had no history of children's Sunday schools, since the Orthodox Church didn't have such programs. Abby worked very hard to put together a program for our church kids. The evangelical church where we rented space also had lots of kids. Could we join them for Sunday School? The pastors expressed openness to the idea.

That arrangement worked for some time and by now Abel was in middle school, when a racial incident rocked our family. Abel had a good school friend named Jeffrey, who he invited to the Wednesday youth group at the evangelical church. Jeffrey was biracial, the child of a Caucasian/African-American couple. One evening when I picked them up Abel seemed very upset. 'I don't want to go back to this group anymore,' he said. 'What happened?' I said. He wouldn't tell me. The next day I ran into the youth pastor because we both had offices in the church. 'Hey, Abel was not happy last night after youth group. Did something happen?' In fact, the youth pastor said, it did. 'Every youth meeting someone is assigned to bring cookies and snacks to eat afterwards, and your boys stole the snacks before the end of the program.' 'Really?' I said: 'Did you see them do it?' 'No,' he said, he didn't. But the other kids, the white kids, had told him that. So, when I got home, I asked Abel 'Did you do this?' 'That's why I'm upset,' Abel said. 'We didn't.' 'Then why would he say so?' 'Pastor said the kids told him and he believes them.'

I was also good friends with the worship pastor so the next day I called and asked if we could have meet. When we got together, I told him what was going on and what did he know? The worship pastor said something that still shocks me to this day. 'Tesfai,' he said. 'Your boys are handsome, you know. We have daughters the same age and in the same group.' 'What does that have to do with anything?' I said. 'Well, some people are not comfortable,' he said. So, they had accused our boys of stealing in order to chase them out of the youth group?

That sent a message to our family. We were not welcome at this church. After that, Abby started taking the boys to the Cathedral of Faith. She would take them Sunday mornings, stay an hour, and then return for our Amharic service at 11am. Friday nights they went to the Cathedral of Faith youth group. Meanwhile, because our church had nothing special for our Ethiopian youth, more of the youth who were Abel and Danny's ages started going to Cathedral of Faith.

How did that work out?

FOUR

Back to Seminary

It's a brilliant Saturday afternoon in July in San Francisco. Pastor Tesfai and Abby have invited their sons, Abel and Daniel, to a BBQ at the Tesema parsonage, a two-story house that adjoins the Addis Kidan Lutheran Church, a turn-of-the-last-century white clapboard Lutheran church with pretty stained-glass windows in San Francisco's Outer Mission District, now reborn as an outreach to the Ethiopian/Eritrean community under Pastor Tesfai's leadership since 2012.

Tesfai grills hamburgers in the backyard. Abby is making wat in the kitchen, a chickpea dish with Berbera spices to make your mouth water or cringe, depending on the strength of your tastebuds. Daniel, the younger son (34) is in a talkative mood. He's engaged to marry Yemeserach, an Ethiopian woman he met while working on his Master's in Public Policy in Belgium. Abel (36) looks more 'Ethiopian', with his head of dreadlocks and gentle smile.

After lunch, our visit with the Tesema Family moves to that most important gesture of Ethiopian hospitality—the Coffee Ceremony. The boys say 'goodbye' and head off for a meet-up with a friend. Abby brings a panful of raw green beans. She's wearing her traditional habesha kemis, a white full-sleeved, floor-length dress with exquisite gold embroidering. She kneels on the living room floor to roast the beans like popcorn, shaking them in a long-handled wok-like pan over an electric grill. They turn a deep chocolate black and the room drips with the strong aroma. She grinds the roasted beans in a clay mortar pot, with a small hand pestle. From there to the pot of water, back on the electric grill. This whole process will take an hour, she says, and while she prepares coffee, she starts the story of the family crisis.

"So, I told Abel we were going to church that morning—he was in middle school—and he said: 'Which church? Your church or my church?' I was horrified. 'How can you say *your church*? Your father is the pastor.' 'So what?' he says. 'I don't understand what my father is preaching. How can it be my church?'

"That's when it first dawned on Abby and me," Tesfai says. "We were building and developing a church our kids could not be a part of. It was a huge shock."

"In fact, we were losing all of our children. All the Ethiopian/Eritrean immigrant kids," Abby says. "It was the same in every house."

"Abby and I would talk about this. We're building a congregation of Ethiopians. It's a good thing. We like it. We're happy. And our kids are not. About that time, I was preparing a sermon on John 4—the Samaritan Woman and Jesus Story.

"She says to Jesus: 'Are you greater than our father Jacob, who gave us this well?' She was paying Jacob a huge compliment for making the well available to her people, for maybe thirty or forty generations. Something clicked in my mind this time as I read the story. The well and our Ethiopian church are one and the same. The well gave life-giving water to her people for generations. And our Ethiopian church has given life-giving water to generations of people. But my children can't enjoy the water we offer them. It's freshwater and they are like tropical fish that can only live in saltwater. This church is going to end when we die.

"No one else in our church seemed to see this as a problem. Even other pastors I knew across the country— none of them voiced this as a problem. It seemed to just be me and Abby. Around that time, I spoke with this fellow Kroeker, from the L.G. Church. He said of the kids who grew up with him in his church, nearly all of them had just disappeared. The reason, he thought, was his church's use of German into the 1960s, which the parents all understood, and the kids didn't. A bell went off in my head. This is our story. I began to see that the future of our church was in jeopardy. An ethnic language specific ministry like ours was a dead end. We needed to begin to think about ministry in

English, both for our kids' sake and for the legacy of the ethnic church.

"During this period of discovery, I met Pastor Bob Newton and we became friends. He was pastoring a Lutheran Church in downtown San Jose. We started praying together and meeting once a week for breakfast. I shared with him our challenge.

"'Your problem is cross-cultural,' Dr. Newton said. 'Right now, your church is one culture. But your children are more American than they are Ethiopian. You should think about developing a ministry that reaches across the culture gap, across the generation gap.' He'd been on the mission field in the Philippines for fifteen years. He was an educator. 'Think about going back to school and getting some training in cross-cultural ministry,' he said. He offered to connect me with key folks at Concordia Seminary/Fort Wayne, where he had worked as an educator with their Mission Program.

"I went home and shared all this with Abby. Then we shared it with the leaders of our church. 'I need to go back to school. I'm hoping to learn something that will help our kids,' I told them. "Maybe it's even bigger than that. Maybe this is something all first-generation churches are facing.'"

The coffee bubbles up and lifts the straw lid on the little pitcher over the hotplate. Abby tilts the pitcher and the pungent black gold falls into four handle-less cups on the tray. She comes around with the tray to serve them, but she's still focused on our conversation. "I don't think the elders understood the challenge or the crisis that we felt inside ourselves. Our sons were mid and late teens by now. Their children were still toddlers," she says. "They thought: our kids will pick up the language and they'll be like us!"

"Even the concept of first-generation and second-generation did not make sense to them." Tesfai says. "They saw my plan as my desire to get a PhD behind my name.

"That same year, 2003, Bob Newton got elected president of our district. He stopped pastoring, but he introduced me to Mike Gibson, the pastor of Mt. Olive Lutheran Church in Milpitas. Gibson was very mission-minded and a very gifted preacher. At the time, his congregation was mostly Caucasian white, and he saw how the Bay Area was rapidly growing ethnically diverse. We became friends. I started praying with him. And we talked about: maybe we can join these two churches; maybe the Ethiopian church and your church could collaborate and together plant another church which will be multi-ethnic. Your church could contribute six or eight core families and our church could do the same. We were both enthusiastic about the concept. As our discussions progressed, I brought along my leaders. And being a senior pastor, out of respect or maybe because they felt I had authority to decide such stuff, nobody questioned my direction. There was no No but no strong Yes either.

"I don't believe the leaders caught the vision, nor did they feel the burden," Abby says. "They hadn't faced the challenge yet. They were just starting families. Our kids were older. Abel was done with high school in 2001. Danny finished in 2003."

"They did not say No," Tesfai says. "Neither was there huge excitement about a multi-ethnic church. Still, it looked like we had arrived at a consensus. I communicated the plan to the congregation, and they supported it. I would remain their senior pastor, traveling back and forth from Ft. Wayne every couple months until I finished the course work.

"I had trained two people from our congregation to be associate pastors. They were already working as pastors under me. So, we made the decision to go to Concordia Seminary in Fort Wayne, Indiana. We would take up residence in Fort Wayne because the program required a residence for the first year of studies. Before I left, I made sure that the elders and assistant pastors connected with Gibson and Newton."

Abby breaks in to add the family details. "Abel had already left home on his own. Danny had just finished high school, so he came with us to Fort Wayne."

"Shortly we began to hear of some change of minds in the church," Tesfai says. "Some of the leaders were saying: Maybe it was not a good idea to pursue this multi-ethnic idea. I wish we could have had an open discussion, but it happened without me present. The leaders contacted Pastor Gibson and told him they were not going to go through with the project. In fact, I heard about their decision from Mike Gibson before I heard it from them.

"I came back and told them directly how disappointed I was about their decision. But the project was ended.

"However, my conversation with Mike Gibson continued, without the church. Mike wanted us to come back in 2006 and work with the original idea—planting a third church in the San Jose area that would appeal to Hispanics and the multiethnic group of people living in that neighborhood. So, as I continued my studies at Concordia, we continued to make plans to do that, three or four years out.

"Little did we know, our journey to a real multi-ethnic, cross-cultural ministry was only beginning. Mike Gibson was going to take a new position in Los Angeles and move away. I was going to come down with cancer."

PART TWO

Research

FIVE

The Multicultural Church and God's Word

In this book I take a deep dive into the life and challenges of Generations 1.5 and 2.0 Ethiopians and Eritreans in the United States. After interviewing twenty-five young Ethiopians during my doctoral research, I report the findings in '25 Young Ethiopians Speak', at the end of this section of the book. Every one of my interviewees used the word 'bicultural' to describe him/herself. Two cultures: the immigrant world of their fathers and mothers and the world and culture of their new home, the U.S.A.—the children need to sort out where they belong. They negotiate where they fit in the two cultures. They must negotiate language, their social lives, politics, food, music, education, in fact, their whole worldview. The culture of the parental home mixes with the culture of American society in them. The result? They turn out quite different people from their parents.

We should expect that any church that wishes to attract them will also differ sharply from the church of their parents, the church in which most of the children grew up.

This book agrees: immigrant children experience enormous challenges as followers of Jesus Christ in the New Land. They also have in hand a very unique opportunity to spread the good news of the Gospel in the Western World. This book offers Biblical and missiological insights to guide church leaders as they disciple their offspring and cast the vision of God's Kingdom. Although my focus is Ethiopian and Eritrean immigrants in the U.S., my conversations with immigrant pastors from other parts of the globe convince me that these insights may apply to most, if not all, recent immigrants from the Third World who are seeking to develop Christian ministry for their children.

We learn from missiology—the study of the mission of the church, especially the character and purpose of missionary work—that churches are not just spiritual entities. They are cultural organisms. Just as the incarnate Christ revealed Himself and served in the clothing of Jewish culture and tradition two thousand years ago, the church has adopted the shape of every culture and people group in which it finds itself, over the centuries of its existence. We find English, German, Spanish, Chinese, Swahili and Amharic churches. The difference between these churches is greater than language. These churches also have tribal, racial, and geographical characteristics. The Church of the Generation 1.5 and 2.0 immigrant population will not be an exception. A church that wishes to connect and minister to this population must reflect elements of language, race and ethnicity that ring true to this generation's social and cultural identity.

What does the world of a bicultural person look like?

Ken Fong, in his fascinating book, *Pursuing the Pearl* (Judson Press, 1999), offers a metaphor I find very helpful. Pastor Fong writes out of his own experience as a third-generation Chinese immigrant, born and raised in Sacramento, California. In the section he calls 'The Immigration Timeline' he compares the first, second and third generation immigrant to fresh-water, bay-water, and saltwater fish, respectively. The first-generation immigrant, he says, is like a fish in freshwater, such as the bass. Freshwater flows from the mountains, hills and the land into the sea. He compares the fish of these waters to the first-generation population—the brave, the adventuresome, seeking new opportunity and tearing themselves loose from the ancestral land to migrate to the sea, which he identifies as America. The bay, he says, is an offshore body (not as distant as the ocean, a water close to the land, yet connected to the larger sea), a place where fresh and saltwater mix. The 1.5 and 2.0 generation children are like the salmon, which lives and thrives in the brackish water of the bay. He compares the third generation, his own, to the cod, a saltwater or deep-sea fish. Like the cod, the third generation is born, lives and dies in the host culture. The bass cannot live and thrive in saltwater and in the same way, the cod cannot live in freshwater. The salmon, however, can live in both freshwater and saltwater, yet the place where it thrives is the bay, where rivers and ocean intersect to form a vast pool of brackish water, a mixture of fresh and salt.

Although Generation 1.5 and 2.0 immigrant children can swim in all three cultures, to some degree, they thrive in a mixed social and cultural environment. And we cannot forget that sooner or later they will rear third generation immigrants who will continue the path of complete integration into American society. "What kind of social and cultural environment suits these immigrant children?" The answer is "a multiethnic and multicultural environment."

Lucky for us, this came as no surprise discovery to the God of the Bible or to the Early Church. The Bible offers guidance and even gives examples of what cross-cultural ministry looks like.

With that overview, let's turn to the Bible. I'll turn first to the Book of Acts, and then look at mission theory as we propose practical steps to develop ministries to these unique people.

A SURVEY OF ACTS, CHAPTERS 1:1–11:26: MULTICULTURAL MINISTRY IN THE EARLY CHURCH

I am convinced the Bible provides direction for the development of a multiethnic or multicultural ministry. The Holy Spirit has given us an example of such a church in the pages of the Book of Acts, the wonderful story of the birth of the Church.

A Survey of Acts, Chapters One to Seven

The Christian Church roots deeply in the Jewish culture

and people. Our Lord was born a Jew and ministered almost exclusively to First Century Jews. His twelve disciples and early followers were all Jewish. The Twelve voiced concern about the Jewish state before his departure.

> [4] On one occasion, while he was eating with them, he gave them this command: "Do not leave Jerusalem, but wait for the gift my Father promised, which you have heard me speak about. [5] For John baptized with water, but in a few days you will be baptized with the Holy Spirit." [6] So when they met together, they asked him, "Lord, are you at this time going to restore the kingdom to Israel?" [7] He said to them: "It is not for you to know the times or dates the Father has set by his own authority. [8] But you will receive power when the Holy Spirit comes on you; and you will be my witnesses in Jerusalem, and in all Judea and Samaria, and to the ends of the earth." (Acts 1:4–8)[4]

From this text it is hard to imagine the disciples were ever considering a ministry outside their Jewish circles. Luke, the author of Acts, captures their fixation on the Jewish nation. But Jesus calls for a worldwide Church. Jesus' declaration that his disciples will go to the ends of the earth with the message of the Gospel stands as a strong critique to any ethnic group that seeks to corral the Gospel within its own ethnic boundaries. Although it took several years before the disciples fulfilled the call to carry the message beyond their ethnic people group, the book of Acts stands as a historic monument to the way the disciples would obey and carry out our Lord's command to them in Acts 1:8.

The Book of Acts tells us the gospel was already crossing cultural lines in the earliest days of the church. The very first mission act of God the Holy Spirit crossed cultural barriers. Notice the Holy Spirit at work in Acts Two.

> Now there were staying in Jerusalem God-fearing Jews from every nation under heaven. When they heard this sound, a crowd came together in bewilderment, because each one heard them speaking in his own language. Utterly amazed, they asked: "Are not all these men who are speaking Galileans? Then how is it that each of us hears them in his own native language? Parthians, Medes and Elamites; residents of Mesopotamia, Judea and Cappadocia, Pontus and Asia, Phrygia and Pamphylia, Egypt and the parts of Libya near Cyrene; visitors from Rome (both Jews and converts to Judaism); Cretans and Arabs-we hear them declaring the wonders of God in our own tongues!" Amazed and perplexed, they asked one another, "What does this mean?" (Acts 2:5–11)

Commentators define Luke's technical phrase, "God-fearing Jews," as people of Jewish faith and ethnicity who have come to celebrate Pentecost from areas of the world beyond the borders of the Jewish state. John Stott writes:

> Luke's emphasis is on the international nature of the crowd which collected. They were all God-fearing Jews, and they were all staying in Jerusalem. Yet they had not been born there; they came from the dispersion, from every nation under heaven. ... He was speaking, as the biblical writers normally did, from his own horizon... and was referring to the Greco-Roman world situated round the Mediterranean basin, indeed to every nation in which there were Jews.[5]

Luke highlights the international nature of the crowd and the extraordinary action the Holy Spirit takes as he announces the message of the Gospel and calls all people to repent, regardless of their cultural identities. The text following these verses shows thousands converting, through the preaching of the Apostle Peter, and tells us these new believers organized themselves for worship and fellowship through the teaching and guidance of the Apostles. Does God's action show that he sees all human culture and language as equal and useful? It seems so. As DeYoung, Emerson, Yancey and Kim write, the church that the Holy Spirit created on the day of Pentecost was multicultural.

On the day of Pentecost, the Jerusalem congregation grew from 120 Galilean Jews to over 3,000 multicultural and multilingual Jews (Acts 2:41). Several thousand more were added in the days that followed (Acts 4:4, 5:14, 6:7). The church was multicultural and multilingual from the first moment of its existence.[6]

Verses 5ff suggest the converts were all Jews, yet Luke does not gloss over their cultural and linguistic differences. Each group heard God's Word in their native language. God's decision to reach out to these people in languages that they understood or preferred says something important about the method God uses to reach people, when it comes to language and culture. Although these individuals all appear to be Jews, birth and upbringing in a different part of the world has given them a different cultural experience than their Jewish co-ethnics born and raised in the Jewish nation. God chose to respect these other languages and cultures.

There is a critical lesson here for first-generation immigrant churches. Most first-generation pastors and parents hesitate to teach their children the Bible in English. Some believe using the Amharic Bible will couple learning of language and culture with spiritual truth. So, these pastors advocate for the use of the ethnic language Bible. Most organize ministry to their children in English with many reservations, although their children speak and read the ethnic language poorly and resources for children in the ethnic language are extremely limited. In the Ethiopian Christian community, children graduating from high school are expected to join the first-generation ethnic language congregation. First-generation pastors and parents fail to recognize that, although their children are ethnically Ethiopians, like Ken Fong's salmon, they swim more proficiently in English waters. This text makes clear that God's strategy to reach people is to appeal to them in their native language and culture.

Acts Six continues God's clear intention to build a church that is multicultural. In this chapter Luke records the Enemy's attempt to disrupt the multicultural unity of this community.

> [1] In those days when the number of disciples was increasing, the Grecian Jews among them complained against the Hebraic Jews because their widows were being overlooked in the daily distribution of food. [2] So the Twelve gathered all the disciples together and said, "It would not be right for us to neglect the ministry of the word of God in order to wait on tables. [3] Brothers, choose seven men from among you who are known to be full of the Spirit and wisdom. We will turn this responsibility over to them [4] and will give our attention to prayer and the ministry of the word." [5] This proposal pleased the whole group. They chose Stephen, a man full of faith and of the Holy Spirit; also, Philip, Procorus, Nicanor, Timon, Parmenas, and Nicolas from Antioch, a convert to Judaism. [6] They presented these men to the apostles, who prayed and laid their hands on them. [7] So the word of God spread. The number of disciples in

Jerusalem increased rapidly, and a large number of priests became obedient to the faith. (Acts 6:1–7)

Note that the Apostles did not deal with the problem by proposing the group separate along cultural and linguistic lines. Rather, they proposed an administrative remedy that safeguarded the multicultural character of the new church. Francis Dubose, examining how the book of Acts dealt with cultural divisiveness, says, "The book of Acts recognizes these differences in cultural reality, but it does not cater to it."[7] John Stott goes further in showing that the difference between the two groups was more than language. He writes,

What exactly was the identity of these two groups [*Hellenistai* and *Hebraioi*]? It has usually been supposed that they were distinguished from each other by a mixture of geography and language. That is, the *Hellenistai* came from the diaspora, had settled in Palestine, and spoke Greek, while the *Hebraioi* were natives of Palestine and spoke Aramaic. This is an inadequate explanation, however. Since Paul called himself *Hebraios*, in spite of the fact that he came from Tarsus and spoke Greek, the distinction must go beyond origin and language to culture. In this case the *Hellenistai* not only spoke Greek but thought and behaved like Greeks, while the *Hebraioi* not only spoke Aramaic but were deeply immersed in Hebrew culture.[8]

Although they were all Jews, the newborn community of Jesus-followers were not one culture. We don't know conclusively that these groups worshiped sometimes as separate groups, while remaining one worshiping community, yet it is not difficult to imagine it. The creation of a seven-man leadership arrangement suggests plural leadership within the larger community. Verse Three tells how this came about. "Brothers, choose seven men from among you who are known to be full of the Spirit and wisdom. We will turn this responsibility over to them." Were these men chosen only for the task of food distribution? If we assume they are just table boys, we miss the message of the passage. These men possessed exceptional spiritual gifts and abilities. These are leaders capable of teaching and performing miracles. Stephen's address in the face of opposition in Acts Seven and Philip's ministry in Samaria prove this point.

In fact, this text may be uncovering an attempt to create a parallel worshiping group, similar to the one we read about in Verse Nine.

Opposition arose, however, from members of the Synagogue of the Freedmen (as it was called)—Jews of Cyrene and Alexandria as well as the provinces of Cilicia and Asia. These men began to argue with Stephen.

Stott in his commentary says the following regarding "Synagogue of the Freedmen":

The 'freedmen' were freed slaves and their descendants. But who were the Jews from Cyrene, Alexandria, Cilicia and Asia? Some think that they composed four distinct synagogues, with the freedmen making a fifth. Others think two, three or four synagogues are in mind. But perhaps it is best to understand with the NIV that Luke is referring to only one synagogue (for the word is in the singular). The NEB also takes it in this way, describing the synagogue as 'comprising' people from the four places mentioned. Because they had been freed from slavery, they must have been foreign Jews who had now come to live in Jerusalem. Perhaps those from Cilicia even included Saul of Tarsus.[9]

In describing the need for a synagogue for Greek speakers, DeYoung, Emerson, Yancey and Kim write, "Many of the Jews who migrated to Jerusalem from the Diaspora spoke Greek. They worshiped in synagogues for Greek speakers and read from a Greek translation of scriptures, the Septuagint.[10]

It appears that the Jews identifying as Freedmen hailed from different parts of the Mediterranean. They had their own synagogue, which suggests the idea of a multicultural community of people from different regions predates the church and was already part of the Jewish experience.

The persecution that led to the dispersion was initiated by this community (*Hellenistai*), and not by *Hebraioi*

Jews. This point alone suggests strong contact between the Christian *Hellenistai* and Jewish *Hellenistai*. Is it possible that the Christian *Hellenistai* had belonged to this group in the past (the Synagogue of the Freedmen) and perhaps still associated with them for the purpose of outreach, just as the Apostles (in Acts 3, 4, and 5) frequented the Temple for the purpose of outreach?

It does not seem far-fetched to me to think that the controversy in Acts 6:1–6 roots in an attempt to create a parallel Christian community similar to the Freedmen Synagogue.

Just as those Jews—both *Hellenistai* and *Hebraioi*—undoubtedly joined together in worship at the Temple, we may suppose the Christian *Hellenistai* and *Hebraioi* Jews also had separate worshiping communities as well. I believe the controversy in Acts Six is about more than the distribution of food. The evidence is the creation of a parallel leadership team in charge of the groups, with the Apostles of Christ leading and binding together these groups. The multicultural character of the Church appears to be as old as its homogeneous character.

A Survey of Acts, Chapters 8:1–11:18

Beginning in Chapter Eight, Luke narrates the dispersion[11] of Christians that followed the death of Stephen and the first move of the Gospel into other regions of the world. We see Jesus' marching orders in Acts 1:8 getting fulfilled as Luke tells the story of Philip's ministry in Samaria, the Ethiopian

Eunuch, Azotus and Caesarea (Acts 8). The apostles Peter and John join Philip in his ministry in Samaria and later Peter travelled to Lydda, Sharon and Joppa (Acts Nine). Acts Ten tells how God altered Peter's travel plans and he finds himself ministering to a Gentile—God forbid!—a Roman centurion named Cornelius and his household in Caesarea. From Caesarea, the gospel travels from its Jewish roots into Gentile territory, leapfrogging cultural lines and national borders. The most astonishing story of multicultural ministry is still on the horizon, in the important city of Antioch.

One way to visualize the fulfilment of Acts 1:8 is by graphing it like this:

Acts 1:8	Geography	Ethnicity	Culture
Jerusalem	Home	Similar	Similar/Different
Judea	Semi-distant	Similar	Similar
Samaria	Distant	Semi-similar	Semi-similar
Ends of the Earth (Antioch & Beyond)	Very Distant	Similar/Different	Similar/Different

This table shows the challenge the first disciples faced as they took the message of the Gospel out, in obedience to their Lord's commandment in Acts 1:8. Row One—home base—is Jerusalem, a mostly Jewish audience. True, there were Romans living in Jerusalem too, and maybe other non-Jewish nationalities, but Luke does not tell us of any ministry directed to people other than Jews. However, as we saw in the discussion on Acts Two and Six, the disciples did minister to Jews from other cultural and linguistic backgrounds. Therefore, the ministry had a multicultural flavor (some were *Hellenistai*), although the people reached were Jews.

Row Two is Judea—this includes Jerusalem and towns around it. For this reason, moderate travel (on foot, of course) was required. Peter's travel to Azotus and Joppa are examples of travel within Judea. In Acts 9:31, even prior to the recorded visit by Peter to the area, the Church was growing in Judea, Galilee and Caesarea: "Then the churches throughout Judea, Galilee and Samaria enjoyed a time of peace. It was strengthened and encouraged by the Holy Spirit, it grew in numbers, living in the fear of the Lord." Moreover, Acts 11:1 clearly states that people throughout Judea heard the message. We observe no groundbreaking news here, because this was ministry to a people with similar ethnic heritage and culture.

Row Three is Samaria—a region at least culturally semi-distant to that of Judea and Galilee. Here the disciples encountered people who were ethnically cousins, due to the common ancestry that Jews and Samaritans shared, but semi-similar in religious and cultural history. Peter's ministry at Cornelius' house was the first recorded truly Gentile mission; however, it appears to be a one-off and symbolic, as it becomes a point of discussion as the Church debated ministry to the Gentiles in Acts Fifteen. The ministry took place in Caesarea, in the home of a Gentile, a semi-distant experience for Peter. We do not read of any subsequent attempt by the apostles (including Peter) to include this newly emerging Christian group within the larger Messianic Jewish community. Luke's record of Peter's defense of his ministry in Caesarea (Acts 11:1–18) falls short of any plan or attempt to continue ministry to this group, indicating that the church was not fully ready to receive Gentiles into their community at this point in time.

True multicultural targeting of people of other ethnicities and cultures first appears in the city of Antioch (Row Four). The Antioch ministry crossed all boundaries; geographically it was beyond the territories of Palestine, ethnically it included non-Jews.

Luke, describing the Antioch outreach, wants to make sure his readers see that the Antioch outreach crossed the same ethnic and cultural boundaries that Pentecost had, but then a big step further—it became truly international or universal in its goals. Acts 11:19–26 reports:

> [19] Now those who were scattered because of the persecution that took place over Stephen traveled as far as Phoenicia, Cyprus, and Antioch, and they spoke the word to no one except Jews. [20] But among them were some men of Cyprus and Cyrene who, on coming to Antioch, spoke to the Hellenists also, proclaiming the Lord Jesus. [21] The hand of the Lord was with them, and a great number became believers and turned to the Lord. [22] News of this came to

the ears of the church in Jerusalem, and they sent Barnabas to Antioch. [23] When he came and saw the grace of God, he rejoiced, and he exhorted them all to remain faithful to the Lord with steadfast devotion; [24] for he was a good man, full of the Holy Spirit and of faith. And a great many people were brought to the Lord. [25] Then Barnabas went to Tarsus to look for Saul, [26] and when he had found him, he brought him to Antioch. So it was that for an entire year they met with the church and taught a great many people, and it was in Antioch that the disciples were first called "Christians."

Why was Antioch so suited for this next step in the development of a multicultural church? Antioch itself was multicultural. Stott, describing the city in his commentary, notes the following:

> The new outreach took place in Antioch, Luke tells us, and no more appropriate place could be imagined, either as the venue for the first international church or as the springboard for the world-wide Christian mission. The city was founded in 300 BC by Seleucus Nictor, one of Alexander the Great's generals. He named it after his father Antiochus, and its port, fifteen miles west along the navigable river Orontes, 'Selucia' after himself. Over the years it became known as 'Antioch the Beautiful' because of

its fine buildings, and by Luke's day was famous for its long, paved boulevard, which ran from north to south and was flanked by a double colonnade with trees and fountains. Although it was a Greek city by foundation, its population, estimated as at least 500,000, was extremely cosmopolitan. It had a large colony of Jews, attracted by Seleucus' offer of equal citizenship, and Orientals too from Persia, India and China, earning it another of its names, 'the Queen of the East.' Since it was absorbed into the Roman Empire by Pompey in 64 BC and became the capital of the imperial province of Syria (to which Cilicia was later added), its inhabitants included Latins as well. Thus Greeks, Jews, Orientals, and Romans formed the mixed multitude of what Josephus called 'the third city of the empire,' after Rome and Alexandria.[12]

With this background, we can now study the evolution of ministry in Acts 11:19–26.

[19] Now those who were scattered because of the persecution that took place over Stephen traveled as far as Phoenicia, Cyprus, and Antioch, and they spoke the word to no one except Jews.

The Gospel was already achieving breakthroughs prior to the outreach in Antioch. Philip ministered in Samaria, baptized the Ethiopian Eunuch, and then went to Azotus in Judea and Caesarea, preaching the Gospel in Chapter Eight. In Acts Nine, Saul, soon to be called by his Greek name, 'Paul,' a chief persecutor of Christ-followers, converts and begins to preach in Damascus. He contacts the apostles in Jerusalem and preaches to Grecian Jews (Acts 9:29), and from there returns to his hometown, Tarsus, by way of Caesarea.

From 9:32–11:18 Luke writes about the Apostle Peter's movements in the nearby towns of Judea and Caesarea. In Chapter Eight, Luke has already told us that Peter, together with John, has visited Samaria after the successful ministry of Philip. The Apostles were busy in Palestine, spreading the Good News of Jesus and establishing churches. Still, Luke's placement of the Antioch story right after the story of Peter's ministry in Acts Ten and his defense of that ministry in Acts 11:1–18 is intriguing. Luke intends to show progression— first Jerusalem, then Judea and Samaria and now the ends of the earth (that is, beyond Palestine). It sounds like Acts 1:8, on the march!

In the Acts 11:19–26 passage, Luke begins by telling us that the disciples scattered throughout the region (Phoenicia, Cyprus and Antioch). However, a new twist in witnessing appears in Antioch. In 11:19, Luke notes, "Now those who had been scattered by the persecution in connection with Stephen traveled as far as Phoenicia, Cyprus and Antioch, telling the message only to Jews." So far, it sounds like same-old, same-old, a strategy focused on witnessing to Jews *only*.

His use of the word "scatter" foretells a next step in the fulfillment of Acts 1:8.

> [20] But among them were some men of Cyprus and Cyrene who, on coming to Antioch, spoke to the Hellenists also, proclaiming the Lord Jesus.

Having noted the *"Jews only"* strategy, Luke draws attention next to "on coming to Antioch", probably to highlight the new strategy of mission that will emerge in Antioch. Ralph Earle in *Word Meanings in New Testament* says the following regarding the "Hellenists" of Acts 11:20:

> ... in 6:1 [Hellenists] rather obviously means "Greek speaking Jews." But here [11:20] it almost as clearly means Gentiles. So, some ancient Greek manuscripts have Hellenas, 'Greeks.' Commentators are agreed that it is very difficult to decide between these two different readings. The first edition of the United Bible Societies' Greek New Testament has *Hellenas,* while the third edition has *Hellenistas.* Bruce Metzger suggests that probably the chief objection of modern scholars to *Hellenistas* is the belief that it always means 'Greek-speaking Jews.' But since *Hellenistas* is derived from *Hellenizein,* it means strictly 'one who uses Greek'... whether the person be a Jew or Roman or any other non-Greek must be gathered from the context. ...In the

present passage, where the preponderant weight of the external evidence combines with the strong transcriptional probability in support of Hellenistas, the word is to be understood in the broad sense of "Greek-speaking persons," meaning thereby the mixed population of Antioch in contrast to the *Ioudaioi [Jews]* of verse 19.[13]

John Stott adds:

There would have been nothing remarkable about preaching to Greek-speaking Jews, for it had been going on from the beginning. It would have not called for a special investigation from Jerusalem. ... The context requires us (like most of the church fathers) to take *Hellenistas* as a synonym for *Hellenas* and to translate it 'Greeks,' or pagans.[14]

F. F. Bruce notes:

To this city of Antioch, then came a number of Hellenistic refugees from Jerusalem, including (Luke tells us) some men whose original homes were in Cyprus and Cyrene. The refugees were active propagandists of their faith, although for the most part they confined their propaganda to their fellow-Hellenists—Greek-speaking Jews—but when these men of Cyprus and Cyrene came to Antioch, they conceived the idea of letting the local Greeks, pagans though they were, share in their good news. Large number of those Greeks hailed the good news as something which exactly met their need.[15]

Like a good suspense writer, Luke takes us with him as he develops his story. First it was the 'Jews only' strategy at Antioch. But then, men from Cyrene and Cyprus reached out to people in Antioch regardless of their ethnic background. Cosmopolitan Antioch was ideal for such a ministry. Yes, the people who engaged the non-Jews of Antioch were themselves ethnic Jews who were *Hellenistai*; this is clarified by Luke's statement that these were from Cyrene and Cyprus. Luke evaluates the new ministry approach with an interesting comment:

> [21] The hand of the Lord was with them, and a great number became believers and turned to the Lord.

Something new! Antioch will become the first multicultural church. Description of these believers in Acts 15:1 and Galatians 2:11ff validates the Jewish/Gentile identity mixture of the Antioch Church. But Luke adds: "The hand of the Lord was with them." Does this comment on successful ministry to the Greeks tell us that 'Jews only' ministry had failed in Antioch? Or at least, it didn't show the 'turning the world upside-down success' we will shortly witness as Paul takes the gospel on the road to Gentiles across the Greco-Roman world. No, God did not disapprove ministry to the

Jews. In fact, on their missionary journeys, Paul and his team went first to the Jews in every city they visited. Although a successful multicultural church was planted in Antioch, ethnic-specific ministry, or 'homogeneity' as a missionary approach, does not get abandoned. What does happen is this: God's plan to bless the Gentiles opens the door for the first multicultural church to emerge.

In Verses 22–24, Luke elaborates on this new growing phenomenon and the concern of the leaders in Jerusalem that prompts them to send Barnabas to make sure everything is going right.

> [22] News of this came to the ears of the church in Jerusalem, and they sent Barnabas to Antioch. [23] When he came and saw the grace of God, he rejoiced, and he exhorted them all to remain faithful to the Lord with steadfast devotion; [24] for he was a good man, full of the Holy Spirit and of faith. And a great many people were brought to the Lord.

Of course, the apostles and other leaders in Jerusalem wanted to hear what was happening on the mission front. In Acts 8:14 they had heard about the success of Philip's ministry and sent Peter and John. In Acts 11:1 they had heard Peter's report about the ministry at Cornelius' house. Now when the news reached them about Antioch, Luke tells us, they sent a man by the name of Barnabas. This time they did not send an apostle. Barnabas, who was a *Hellenista* from

Cyprus (Acts 4:36), in turn invited another *Hellenista* by the name of Paul from Tarsus, at a time when all the disciples in Jerusalem harbored suspicions or at least questions, about what was going on up there in Antioch. It appears Barnabas was the right man for the job.

> Bruce comments:
> The leaders of the Jerusalem church at this stage appear to have exercised a general supervision or indeed, control over the spread of the gospel into adjacent territories. ... A delegate was accordingly sent to Antioch to see what was going on. The result might have been disastrous if the wrong type of delegate had been chosen; fortunately, the man who was sent was Barnabas, the "encourager."[16]

Rather than squashing this new multicultural church (verses 23 and 24), Barnabas rejoiced and empowered them to continue to serve God. The result was growth in numbers and the development of a mission center for world outreach. Nonetheless, what happens next is equally important.

> [25] Then Barnabas went to Tarsus to look for Saul, [26] and when he had found him, he brought him to Antioch. So it was that for an entire year they met with the church and taught a great many people, and it was in Antioch that the disciples were first called "Christians."

Just as the selection of the apostles and sending of Barnabas were God-Moves, Barnabas' seeking out (Saul) Paul was equally a God Move. He could have gone to Jerusalem to request another teacher or asked the apostles to send one. Instead, Barnabas seeks out a fellow *Hellenista* (Greek-speaking Jew). Together, this two-man team spent an entire year teaching new believers before the Jerusalem leadership sent them to their next mission in Acts 13:4.

What is the significance of Luke's comment in Verse Six that "it was in Antioch that the disciples were first called 'Christians'"? John Stott says:

> They must have taught about Christ, making sure that the converts knew both the facts and the significance of His life, death, resurrection, exaltation, Spirit-gift, present reign and future coming. It was because the word 'Christ' was constantly on their lips that the disciples were called Christians first at Antioch. Luke has so far referred to them as 'disciples' (6:1), 'saints' (9:13), 'brethren' (1:16; 9:30), 'believers' (10:45), 'those being saved' (2:47) and the people 'of the Way' (9:2). Now it seems to have been the unbelieving public of Antioch, famed for their wit and nicknaming skill, who, supposing that 'Christ' was a proper name rather than a title (the Christ or Messiah), coined the epithet *Christianoi*. ... It marked out the disciples as being above all people, the followers, the servants of Christ.[17]

Earle adds:

A reason for coining the term *Christianoi* is that the Christians in Antioch were viewed as a separate society rather than a section of the Jewish Synagogue.[18]

We find the word 'Christian' only three times in the New Testament. Other than here, the other times we find it are Acts (26:28) and 1 Peter (4:16). In Acts 26:28, we read "then Agrippa said to Paul, 'Do you think that in such a short time you can persuade me to be a *Christian*?'"

This encounter with King Agrippa, while Paul was in prison in Caesarea, suggests that by this date fourteen to fifteen years after his ministry in Antioch, outsiders in places far from Antioch were calling the disciples or followers of Christ 'Christians.' In fact, believers also referred to themselves this way, which may have promoted the usage everywhere. Notice I Peter 4:16: "However, if you suffer as a *Christian*, do not be ashamed, but praise God that you bear that name."

Describing the significance of the 'Christian' label, DeYoung, Emerson, Yancey and Kim write:

The name declared that they made up a social but not an ethnic group. ... The Christians couldn't be classified according to the classification categories of either pagans or Jews. They were both and yet they were neither the one nor the other alone. They were the same and yet they lived differently. They were bound together by a new intimacy and mutual concern that went beyond normal, acceptable behavior within the empire.[19]

In short, a new religious identity, a new community called 'Christians' has arrived on the scene. They are ethnically, socially and culturally inclusive. They are distinct from Jews—their multicultural population, spiritual practice and growth prove it. From now on they will not viewed as a branch of Judaism.

The church in Antioch not only represented a new type of community; it also became a springboard for world mission. What happened in Antioch was a tremendous breakthrough. Next to Pentecost, it stands as the second most important event for the spread of the Gospel and the fulfillment of the promise of Pentecost. From here on, Luke narrates the viral spread of the Gospel into Gentile lands and the planting of churches across the Roman Empire (Acts 13:1–21:16 records Paul's three missionary journeys out of Antioch). The missionary activities in these chapters show a similar mission strategy to that of Antioch; that is, first to the Jews and then to the Gentiles (Acts 26:20). Following that model, the Christian communities that sprang up everywhere were not first defined by ethnicity. DeYoung, Emerson, Yancey and Kim call it the Antioch Model:

> The Antioch congregation became the model for the expansion of the church in the first century. The foremost

initiator of new congregations in this period—the Apostle
Paul—was mentored and sent forth by the leadership of
the Antioch congregation. The congregations founded by
Paul and his coworkers often started in a fashion similar
to that of Antioch. They preached first to Jews and then
to Gentiles. ... We do not know how the evangelism
effort moved forward in each place where Paul preached
and initiated congregations. Nor can we say for sure
that every congregation included both Jews and Gentiles.
Some areas didn't have Jewish population. But we can
observe the inclusion of both Gentiles and Jews in most
locales...[20]

They quote F. F. Bruce, who states the remarkable,
previously unthinkable nature of the emerging church, "The
idea that a church planted by Paul comprised separate Jewish
and Gentile sections is antecedently improbable."[21]

The Dispersion or Scattering

It is important to dig deeper, at this point, to understand
what Paul means when he talks of 'scattering' in Acts
8:1. The people who arrived in Antioch were among the
dispersed. Acts 11:19 begins by saying, "[19] Now those who
had been scattered by the persecution that broke out when
Stephen was killed traveled as far as Phoenicia, Cyprus
and Antioch, spreading the word only among Jews." The
Greek word "Diaspora" is made up of two words; **dia** which
means "throughout," and **speiro** translated "to sow seed."

It literally translates to *scatter abroad, to disperse.* In the case of Verse 19 it means *"being scattered." This* is the same word that Luke uses earlier in Acts 8:1 to describe the scattering of the followers of Christ.

The image presented by "scattering" is the farmer, who scatters or sows seed, in the hope of getting a good harvest. In addition to this agricultural sense, 'scattering seed' is also used in the physiological sense. **Sperma,** translated 'seed,' while referring often to plants, as in the Parable of the Weeds, Matthew 13:24), also describes human or animal semen (*sperm, seed*) and can refer to human descendants (*offspring, posterity, children*), as in Mk 12.19. Sperma is used figuratively in the concept of a remnant from which to build a new lineage (Rom 9.29); and as a principle of life implanted by the Spirit (*imparted nature*) as in First John 3.9.[22] The word **sperma** is related to **speiro,** the root word for 'scattered' in Acts 11:19. The Bible Works 5 Software Lexicon defines it as:

> *Sowing seed, scatter* (Matt 6.26), with the participle as a substantive o` **speiron** *the sower* (Matt 13.3). Metaphorically it can refer to (a) telling the Word of God, spreading the gospel as divine seed (Mk 4.14); (b) of the natural human body as destined for resurrection (1Cor. 15.42–44); (c) acting in ways that will bring multiplication.[23]

In these cases, scattering carries the concept of purpose, for the production or bringing forth of life.

In contrast, the other commonly used Greek word for scattering in both the New Testament and the Septuagint (the Greek translation of the Old Testament and therefore, the Scripture used by the New Testament Christians) is **skorpizw,** which also literally means *scatter, disperse.* It is more commonly used in connection with God's judgment. The *Theological Dictionary of the New Testament*[24] suggests that **skorpizw** has a somewhat negative connotation. Kittle references the use of the word in the Septuagint, citing God's judgment on his enemies (2 Sam 22:15); the judgment on Jerusalem in Ezek 5:1ff, a scattering that includes fire and sword; and its usage in Zechariah—"the sheep will be scattered when the shepherd is smitten" (Zech 13:7ff). In the New Testament, the word is used by Jesus, when he says those who do not gather with him 'scatter', as in hindering God's word (Matt 13:30; Luke 11:23). In John 10:1ff the good shepherd gathers and protects the flock, whereas the wolf 'scatters,' kills, and destroys.

Despite the frequent association of the word (**skorpizw**) with God's judgment, the Septuagint also uses **diaspeirw** to describe judgment. Here are a few examples:

Septuagint: Leviticus 26:33 "And I will scatter you among the nations, and the sword shall come upon you and consume you; and your land shall be desolate, and your cities shall be desolate."

Septuagint: Deuteronomy 4:27 "And the Lord shall scatter you among all nations, and ye shall be left few in number among all the nations, among which the Lord shall bring you."

Septuagint: Deuteronomy 28:64 "And the Lord thy God shall scatter thee among all nations, from one end of the earth to the other; and thou shalt there serve."

But Luke chose to use **diaspeiro** to describe the dispersion of God's people every time he wanted to communicate scattering with the purpose of producing life and **skorpizo** when he wanted to speak about destruction and disintegration. He speaks of scattering seven times in his writing; three times in his Gospel and four times in Acts. In the Gospel he uses **skorpizo** to describe God's action of scattering the proud and lifting up the humble (Luke 1:51, 52). This verse is part of Mary's song, 'the Magnificat,' and she sings about God's judgment on the rulers of the earth, his destruction of those who oppose God and His rule. In Luke 11:23 Jesus says, "he who is not with me is against me, and he who doesn't gather with me scatters." **Skorpizo** here describes someone who hinders God's work and the advance of his Kingdom. In Acts 5:37, Luke uses the same word in Gamaliel's speech to the Sanhedrin, who wish to judge the apostles. Gamaliel tells how would-be messiahs will fail, their followers will be scattered, and their purpose will be destroyed or failed. The Greek word Luke uses to describe the end of these wannabe messiahs in Acts 5:38 is **katalythesetai**. The root word is kataluo, a compound word made from 'kata' (meaning 'down') and luo (meaning 'to lose, break or dissolve'). The word is often translated *destroyed*. The two words merged depict a sense of being overthrown completely or destroyed. Jesus uses **katalythesetai** in his Sermon on the Mount, "Do not think that I have come to abolish the Law or the Prophets...." (Matt 5:17) Luke uses it in his Gospel when he records Jesus' prophecy of the destruction of the temple, "As for what you see here, the time will come when not one stone will be left on another; every one of them will be thrown down." (Luke 21:6). He again uses it in the accusation made against Stephen in Acts 6:14: "For we have heard him say that this Jesus of Nazareth will destroy this place and change the customs Moses handed down to us."

My point is to show that it is **skorpiow**, not **diaspeiro**, is the word Luke uses whenever he describes scattering in the sense of destruction.

The only time the word **skorpizo** appears to have a positive sense in the New Testament is Matthew 25:26, the Parable of the Talents:

> [26] His master replied, 'You wicked, lazy servant! So, you knew that I harvest where I have not sown and gather where I have not scattered seed?'

This is the only instance in the New Testament when both espeira 'to sow' which is derives from **speiro,** the root word for **diaspora,** and **skorpizo,** meaning *scattered*, are found together. Perhaps the reason it appears positive here is its association with the word **speiro**, which as we already know refers primarily to the 'sowing of seed.'

Let's look at another variant for **diaspeiro**, the word **peiron,** which Luke uses as he tells the story of the Parable of the Sower (Luke 8:5) **diasparente**, used three times in Acts 8:1, 4 and 11:19. His choice of **diasparente** in these verses and not **skorpizo** as in Luke 1:51; 11:23; Acts 5:37 tells us this scattering is intentional. The "Word" is spreading to the far ends of the earth through disciples "scattered" to the ends of the earth (Acts 1:8)—a positive event!

The New Testament shows gradual acceptance of the Dispersion and voluntary migration, even by religious leaders, thereby lessening the pain of scattering, if not completely removing the strong stigma associated with it. In John 7:33–36, where Jesus spoke at the feast of Tabernacles about his death and the fact that he is with them only for a short time, the Jews wondered if his disappearance meant that he would be going to the Jews who were scattered among the Gentiles.

> [35] The Jews said to one another, "Where does this man intend to go that we cannot find him? Will he go where our people live scattered among the Greeks, and teach the Greeks? [36] What did he mean when he said, 'You will look for me, but you will not find me,' and 'Where I am, you cannot come'?"

By the time of Jesus some religious leaders had voluntarily joined or followed the *diaspora* in order to teach and serve these communities in other parts of the world. This, by the way, characterizes immigrant communities today. Where the people go, religious leaders follow.

Although the experience of scattering seems negative from the viewpoint of the natural man, when viewed from a 'God's Kingdom' point of view, it advances God's purpose. The apostle Peter captured this positive understanding of dispersion and gave it meaning for our faith in his letter:

> RSV 1 Peter 1:1 Peter, an apostle of Jesus Christ, To the exiles of the Dispersion in Pontus, Galatia, Cappadocia, Asia, and Bithynia, 2 chosen and destined by God...
>
> NIV 1 Peter 1:1 Peter, an apostle of Jesus Christ, To God's elect, strangers in the world, scattered throughout Pontus, Galatia, Cappadocia, Asia and Bithynia.

Peter addresses the believers scattered across Asia Minor as the Dispersion or Diaspora. He also uses two other words in connection with the Dispersion—'elect'—which carries the idea of being selected or chosen[25] and 'strangers.' 'Stranger' connotes 'one who is temporarily a resident alien'[26], living on a passport, a sojourner. Where the NIV translates 'strangers,' the RSV translates the same word as 'exiles'. Wayne Grudem, in his commentary on First Peter, comments on these translations:

'Exiles' (RSV) is not the best rendering, for no connotation of forced dwelling away from one's homeland is found in the word. Likewise, the rendering 'strangers' (... NIV 'strangers in the world') wrongly suggests that they were not known well by their neighbors...[27]

Let's now look deeper at the concept of 'sojourners' and 'exiles' in Scripture. Grudem compares the experience of Abraham among the Hittites as a sojourner (*parepidemos*, in the Septuagint version of Genesis 23:4, the same word we find in 1 Peter 1:1) with Hebrew 11:13. where the heroes of faith from Abel to Abraham are called sojourners on earth. The writer of Hebrews does not intend to say that they are strangers to their contemporaries.[28] Grudem concludes that a better translation is "those who reside as aliens (NASB), which, though lengthy, captures the idea of temporary residence away from one's homeland, as does the somewhat archaic word 'sojourners'"[29].

The RSV postpones the word 'chosen' to Verse Two, which suggests the exiles had no choice over whether they were scattered or not. Similarly, the NIV separates the words for election, stranger, and scatter with commas, which gives the impression these words describe separate and different qualities of the scattered people of God (as though election had no connection with them being in sojourn or in being scattered). In contrast, the English Standard Version holds together election, exile, and dispersion without commas.

ESV 1 Peter 1:1 Peter, an apostle of Jesus Christ, to those who are elect exiles of the dispersion in Pontus, Galatia, Cappadocia, Asia, and Bithynia,

Without the commas, the election and scattering of the believers as sojourners or temporary resident aliens looks deliberate from God's viewpoint and from the eye of faith.

Nowhere else in Jewish or Christian literature do we find this idea of a sojourner who is 'elect.'[30] And what is the identity of these sojourners? Are they Jews? Jewish followers of Jesus? Gentile followers of Jesus? The *Theological Dictionary of the New Testament* notes this about First Peter 1:1 and James 1:1:

In James 1:1 and 1 Peter 1:1 a question arises whether the authors have in mind Christian Jews, in which case the sense is literal, or Gentile Christians, or Christians in general, in which case it is figurative. In James 1:1 the "twelve tribes" are most likely Christians, who are now the people of God with the heavenly Jerusalem as their home, so that at the present they, too, are dispersed among the nations. If this is the reference, the recipients are simply Christians, both Jews and Gentiles. ...[31]

Grudem agrees:

The phrase 'chosen sojourners' thus becomes a two-word sermon to Peter's readers: they are 'sojourners,' not in an earthly sense (for many no doubt had lived in one city their whole lives), but spiritually: their true homeland is heaven (Philippians 3:20) and any earthly residence therefore temporary.[32]

Regarding the term *diaspora,* or dispersion in First Peter, Grudem says:

> The Dispersion (*diaspora*) was a term used by Greek-speaking Jews to refer to Jewish people 'scattered' throughout the nations, 'dispersed' from their homeland, Israel... Here and in James 1:1, 'Dispersion' refers to Christians, but this does not imply that Peter was writing to Jewish Christians... Rather, the term here has a new spiritual sense, referring to Christians 'dispersed' throughout the world and living away from their heavenly homeland... The word thus reinforces the meaning of 'sojourners' and adds the idea that they are part of a 'world-wide' scattering of Christians.[33]

George Ladd also agrees that the people addressed by Peter were Gentiles. He notes:

> The letter is addressed "to the exiles of the dispersion" in the province of Asia (1:1), but it is clear that these are Gentiles (2:10; 4:3). Probably 1 Peter is a circular letter like Ephesians.[34]

In any case, the concept of Christians as sojourners or living as people on passport in this world is not only a New Testament motif; it is a Biblical motif to describe the elect people of God. Hebrews 11:16: "They were longing for a better country—a heavenly one. Therefore, God is not ashamed to be called their God, for he has prepared a city for them." Such people did not pledge allegiance to a single nation but pledged allegiance first and foremost to God's kingdom, a realm far superior and greater than any country on earth. Did the disciples understand this concept? Notice Luke's description of them in Acts 1:4–8.

[1] In my former book, Theophilus, I wrote about all that Jesus began to do and to teach [2] until the day he was taken up to heaven, after giving instructions through the Holy Spirit to the apostles he had chosen. [3] After his suffering, he showed himself to these men and gave many convincing proofs that he was alive. He appeared to them over a period of forty days and spoke about the kingdom of God. [4] On one occasion, while he was eating with them, he gave them this command: "Do not leave Jerusalem, but wait for the gift my Father promised, which you have heard me speak about. [5] For John baptized with water, but in a few days you will be baptized with the Holy Spirit." [6] So when they met together, they asked him, "Lord, are you at this time going to restore the kingdom to Israel?"

When they heard Jesus' command to stay in Jerusalem to receive the promise (the Holy Spirit), the disciples (at least the Eleven and maybe more) asked Jesus when the Kingdom would be restored to Israel. As Luke tells it, this takes place after Jesus had been teaching them about God's kingdom during his forty days with them after the Resurrection. However, the disciples were fixated on a Jewish kingdom; a return to the glory days of Solomon's kingdom, a time when the world would come to Jerusalem. Where did such a request come from? It represents the ancient desire of All Israel for a turnaround of the shame and humiliation that flowed from the history of the divided kingdom and all the misfortunes and misery Israel had suffered under the boot of world powers—Assyria, Babylon, the Greeks and, now in their day, the Romans. If the Kingdom was restored, would that mean an end to the Jewish Dispersion?

Desire for power, unity and security for one special ethnic group (in this case, the Jews) resembles the Story of the Tower of Babel, which we read in Genesis 11:4, "Then they said, 'Come, let us build ourselves a city, with a tower that reaches to the heavens, so that we may make a name for ourselves and not be scattered over the face of the whole earth.'" Discussing this verse, Rhodes notes:

> Although many interpretations have focused on the presupposed pride "making a name," note what motivates this need for power and recognition: the fear of being scattered across the earth. Afraid of once again being separated and differentiated from one another, humanity presents God with a common

front and a unifying purpose—self-preservation on their own terms. ...This is a self-made unity in which humanity has a "fortress mentality." It seeks to survive by its own resources.[35]

The disciples (in Acts 1) were so obsessed with the thought that the messianic kingdom was about to break through in triumph that they missed what Jesus was teaching about the Kingdom of God.

> [7] He said to them: "It is not for you to know the times or dates the Father has set by his own authority. [8] But you will receive power when the Holy Spirit comes on you; and you will be my witnesses in Jerusalem, and in all Judea and Samaria, and to the ends of the earth."

Jesus' words in Acts 1:7, 8 appear to be a gentle rebuke to his disciples. His plan isn't a new Solomonic Kingdom and annihilation of the Gentile nations. His plan calls for *them* to be scattered. They will be his elect sojourners, dispersing to the far ends of the earth as his witnesses. Did the disciples comprehend this identity as elect sojourners? The first few pages of the book of Acts seem to say NO. Peter's assertion of 'elect sojourner' identity comes much later, after they have been dispersed for years. By the time of Peter's first letter, believers everywhere understood their new God-given identity. It was not an accidental identity. 'Elect sojourners' was an identity chosen for them by God, whether they found themselves away from the land of their birth or if they still lived in the Old Country. 'Elect sojourners' was God's design for them, both Jews and Gentiles. It was their new identity.

We can make the case that Jesus intended His disciples to see themselves as 'elect sojourners' as He taught the Kingdom of God, although his disciples were slow to grasp this. The very first parables Jesus told in Matthew 13 were about the kingdom of God. Leaving aside for now the last three parables in the chapter (the Mustard Seed and the Yeast, the Hidden treasure and the Pearl, and the parable of the Net) I will examine the remaining two parables in this chapter.

In the parable we call "the Parable of the Sower" (Matthew 13:1–23), Jesus compares the growth of the kingdom of God and its expansion by the scattering of the message of the Gospel (the Word of God) to a farmer scattering seed. Depending on the type of soil, some of the seeds do not survive on the ground, some do not take root, and still others get choked. But some seeds return a harvest of thirty, sixty or a hundredfold! The sower and the farmer both indiscriminately scatter the seed in the hope of harvesting a crop. The word used for scatter is 'speirein' in Verse Four, meaning 'to sow' with the purpose of receiving back many-fold; it is part of the word 'diaspeiro' meaning 'to scatter,' which is used for the Dispersion (the scattered people in Acts 8:1, 4 and 1:19). This parable sets the stage for the second parable, commonly known as 'the Parable of the Weeds."

[24] Jesus told them another parable: "The kingdom of heaven is like a man who sowed good seed in his field. [25] But while everyone was sleeping, his enemy came and sowed weeds among the wheat, and went away. [26] When the wheat sprouted and formed heads, then the weeds also appeared. [27] "The owner's servants came to him and said, 'Sir, didn't you sow good seed in your field? Where then did the weeds come from?' [28] "'An enemy did this,' he replied. "The servants asked him, 'Do you want us to go and pull them up?' [29] "'No,' he answered, 'because while you are pulling the weeds, you may root up the wheat with them. [30] Let both grow together until the harvest. At that time I will tell the harvesters: First collect the weeds and tie them in bundles to be burned; then gather the wheat and bring it into my barn.'"... [36] Then he left the crowd and went into the house. His disciples came to him and said, "Explain to us the parable of the weeds in the field." [37] He answered, "The one who sowed the good seed is the Son of Man. [38] The field is the world, and the good seed stands for the sons of the kingdom. The weeds are the sons of the evil one, [39] and the enemy who sows them is the devil. The harvest is the end of the age, and the harvesters are angels. [40] "As the weeds are pulled up and burned in the fire, so it will be at the end of the age. [41] The Son of Man will send out his angels, and they will weed out of his kingdom

everything that causes sin and all who do evil. [42] They will throw them into the fiery furnace, where there will be weeping and gnashing of teeth. [43] Then the righteous will shine like the sun in the kingdom of their Father. He who has ears, let him hear."

We don't need a deep-dive exegesis of this parable and its interpretation to make our point here. I will offer a generalized observation.

Noting the way this parable is usually interpreted, Ladd points out that the "older Protestant scholarship sees identification of the Kingdom with the church."[36] However, in the interpretation given by Jesus, "the field is the world" (verse 38), suggesting that the kingdom is larger than the church, and suggesting the active presence of the Kingdom in the world. And although Verse 41 speaks of "the return of the Son of Man", the purpose of the parable is not first of all to comment on end time events. Discussing the purpose for this parable, Ladd notes:

> The parable of the tares further illustrates the mystery of the kingdom, i.e., its hidden, unexpected presence in the world. ... The coming of the Kingdom, as predicted in the Old Testament and in Jewish apocalyptic literature, would bring the end of the age and inaugurate the Age to come, disrupting human society by the destruction of the unrighteous. Jesus affirms that in the midst of the present age, while

society continues with its intermixture of the good and the bad, before the coming of the Son of Man and the glorious manifestation of the Kingdom of God, the powers of the future age have entered into the world to create "sons of the kingdom," those who enjoy its power and blessing. The kingdom has come, but society is not uprooted. This is the mystery of the Kingdom.[37]

Although the parable informs hearers about end-time events, I believe it is primarily a description of life in God's Kingdom today, while the world is allowed to continue in its present condition—where children of God and unbelievers live side by side. Richard Hays suggests:

The parable of the wheat and the weeds (13:24–30) and its interpretation (13:36–43) suggest that there was an active debate in Matthew's community concerning whether the church should seek to be a community of the pure or whether it should accept a more ambiguous status as *corpus mixtum* awaiting the final judgment.[38]

Whether there was such a debate or not, the parable intends to teach much more than mysteries of eschatological events. The strongest support for this observation comes from Jesus' own words as he concludes his interpretation. He paraphrases the prophet Daniel: "Then the righteous will shine like the sun in the kingdom of their Father...." (Luke 13:43). Daniel 12:3 says: "Those who are wise will shine like the brightness of the heavens, and those who lead many to righteousness, like the stars forever and ever."

Daniel and the Jews of his day experienced national dispersion, the terrible dispersion that Moses predicted in Leviticus and Deuteronomy and by prophets such as Jeremiah, Ezekiel and others. From their vantage point, these prophets talked about it as God's judgment of Israel's disobedience. But by linking the Parable of the Wheat and Weeds to the story of Daniel and his generation, Jesus offers a new meaning to the dispersion or scattering. Unlike the customary interpretation, which focuses on the weeds, Jesus highlights the wheat: "those who lead many to righteousness."

In Daniel Two, Daniel's interpretation of Nebuchadnezzar's dream is followed by the king's statement in Verse 47: "The king said to Daniel, 'Surely your God is the God of gods and the Lord of kings and a revealer of mysteries, for you were able to reveal this mystery.'" After the three Hebrews were thrown into the fiery furnace and came out unharmed in Daniel Chapter Three, the king decrees, Verse 29: "Therefore I decree that the people of any nation or language who say anything against the God of Shadrach, Meshach and Abednego be cut into pieces and their houses be turned into piles of rubble, for no other god can save in this way." In Chapter Four, Nebuchadnezzar tells his subjects, a people from many languages and geographical locations, what the God of Daniel did for him after he was delivered from seven years of living like an animal and then restored to power. He states (4:37), "Now I, Nebuchadnezzar, praise and exalt and glorify the King of heaven, because everything he does is right, and all his ways are just. And those who walk in pride he is able to humble." In Chapter Six, after Daniel was thrown into the Lion's den and emerged unharmed because of God's protection, the king, Darius, amazed at the power and care of the God of Daniel, wrote a decree:

> [25] Then King Darius wrote to all the peoples, nations and men of every language throughout the land: "May you prosper greatly! [26] "I issue a decree that in every part of my kingdom people must fear and reverence the God of Daniel. "For he is the living God and he endures forever; his kingdom will not be destroyed, his dominion will never end. [27] He rescues and he saves; he performs signs and wonders in the heavens and on the earth. He has rescued Daniel from the power of the lions."

We find in the story of Daniel that God's fame and honor was declared and nations and people without opportunity to know the God of Israel came to know him through God's scattered people. By referring to the Book of Daniel in his interpretation of the Parable of the Wheat and the Weeds, Jesus shows how the scattering of God's people in the world to shine like stars will lead many to righteousness. From a movement" because we are describing the way in which a people (tribe, caste, or clan) first becomes Christian.[39]

McGavran then spent seventeen years developing a people movement among the Satnamis caste. About one thousand people came to Christ, fifteen small village churches were planted, and the Gospels were translated into the people's language. In 1958, McGavran resigned from his mission work and proposed to a number of American seminaries the possibility of starting a department focused on the subject of church growth. Fuller Theological Seminary in Pasadena, California, appointed McGavran as the first dean of the School of World Mission in 1965 and he subsequently published the book *Understanding Church Growth* (1970). In the book, he articulated a key feature of his church growth theory, which he called the 'homogeneous unit principle.' He formulated this principle from his experience in India with mass conversions. The HUP reasoned that individuals were more likely to convert to Christianity *en masse* when they share similar demographics.

McGavran defined the Homogeneous Unit and the Homogeneous Church by saying, "The homogeneous unit is simply a section of society in which all the members have some characteristics in common."[40] And, "A homogeneous church unit may be defined as that cluster of congregations of one denomination which is growing in a given homogeneous unit."[41] Later, he articulated the statement that became foundational to the church growth movement, "Men and women like to become Christians without crossing barriers."[42] Elaborating on McGavran's definition, Smith, in his dissertation on the concept of the homogeneous unit in the writings of Donald McGavran, says:

> The homogeneous unit is simply a section of society in which all the members have some characteristics in common. That commonality may be geographical or political, cultural, racial, ethnic or linguistic. It is so elastic that it can expand to fit a complex and varied mix or it can constrict to the point of exclusivism."[43]

However, the case for congregational homogeneity would be strengthened and best articulated by Peter Wagner, who became a key spokesman for the Church Growth Movement, as it became known.

> Homogeneous Units: Try not to allow diverse social and cultural elements to mix on the congregational level any more than necessary. Churches must be built as much as possible within homogeneous units if they are to maintain a sense of community among believers.[44]

In 1979 Wagner developed the idea further in his dissertation, *Our Kind of People*:

> An increasing body of missiological research worldwide and sociological research within America itself indicates that most Christian people meet

together for worship and fellowship within the basic sociological groupings into which they were born. Where Christianity is taking root in different nations and cultures of the world, it seems to develop most vigorously when it is allowed or even encouraged to grow in specific homogeneous units rather than forced to include different groups."[45]

A few years later, in 1981, McGavran emphasized the need to focus on social ties in the context of church growth in North America. Notice:

I am asking, 'Why are some American churches growing? My ...answer is that in devising a growth strategy for their churches, they recognize the social realities and teach these to their members, leaders and task forces. Church growth does not take place in a vacuum. It occurs in an enormously complex society, which is really a kaleidoscope of changing parts. Society is constantly changing... Ethnic enclaves are enormously important... non-growing congregations and denominations refuse to see social realities... Hundreds of exclusive homogeneous units now in America prove that thousands of new churches are needed. American society is not composed of one kind of people... American churches ought to place glowing congregations in every homogeneous unit... Furthermore, most existing American congregations will not actively seek new immigrants and provide the care and linguistic accommodation which they crave.... [46]

Tens of thousands of pastors and missionaries from a hundred mainly evangelical denominations trained with the School of World Mission over the 1970s and 80s. McGavran used statistics research to show that the typical missiological strategy of the time—the mission station—was mostly ineffective in reaching people for Christ. These mission stations were also ineffective as tools to make disciples.

Explaining and Defending the Homogeneous Unit Principle

People feel comfortable within their own race or cultural setting—this fact seems as obvious as Two plus Two Equals Four. However, as the Homogeneous Unit Principle grew in popularity in discussions of church growth in the American Evangelical circles, some missionaries and pastors began to raise questions. Yet an important observation about McGavran's reason for popularizing the principle was because of its value for church growth. Churches using the HUP were growing and how could you argue with statistics that showed growing churches?

The principle is also readily discerned when it comes to pronounced class and racial barriers. It takes no great acumen to see that when marked differences of color, stature, income, cleanliness, and education are present, standard language and disregard class differences multiply. In such, the unifying brotherhood should be stressed and worship in the standard language should become standard.[51]

But a few pages earlier, McGavran warned of potential problems with promoting multiethnic ministry. He writes:

> Integration, before both groups of Christians are ready for it, is often the kiss of death to the weaker party. In other words, segregation is sin because it is an exclusion enforced by one group on another. 'One-people' churches are righteous, since they are the choice of a group as to language and customs and do not come about through a desire to exclude 'inferiors'—quite the contrary.[52]

Are McGavran's qualms about multicultural ministry politically rooted?

> Another reason the element of peoplehood is commonly ignored by Christians is that today the Church in America is fighting a great battle for brotherhood. To many Christians, the establishment of brotherhood among the race is the supreme goal of the Church. They are opposed to segregation in any form. They doubt the validity of any principle which encourages Christians of one class or race to

worship together or form congregations for their particular kind of people.[53]

In summary, both McGavran and Wagner reluctantly leave room for heterogeneous—multicultural—ministry.

Evaluation, Concerns and Criticisms on the Homogeneous Unit Principle

Charles Van Engen puts McGavran's HUP under the microscope in his *Is the Church for Everyone? Planting Multi-Ethnic Congregations in North America*, a book published in Year 2000. In a section titled 'McGavran's Original Intent and Wagner's Concession,' Van Engen evaluates the writings of both men. On the positive side, he notes that in the first edition of *Understanding Church Growth* McGavran listed an urban exception to the HUP in 'metropolitan centers' that are melting pots or cosmopolitan.[54] He also cites McGavran's appointment of Alan Tippet to the School of World Mission as symbolic of his sensitivity to culture and its importance in missions.

> ... McGavran's foundational thought had to do with cultural sensitivity that recognizes what is happening in a given context and responds appropriately. This led him to stress predominantly the matter of cultural differences between groups. But behind this was a profound desire to be "indigenous," to be contextually attuned to the cultural realities of

of the U.S. Census Bureau (African-American, Asian, White, Native American, etc.) simply do not work. Hispanics are sometimes lumped among whites, ignoring places of origin and a host of other ways in which Hispanics differentiate themselves one from another. "Asian" is a catch-all term that is essentially meaningless, given the wide differences between, say the Korean, Chinese (American-born or Overseas-born) Japanese, Taiwanese, or Vietnamese, Thai, Cambodian, Laotian, and so forth.[58]

He adds:

When one gets into generational issues of immigrant families, the second- and third-generations are so culturally dissimilar to their immigrant parents that to lump them into the same "ethnic" categories is to ignore some of the most important features of cultural differences which anthropologists and sociologists would want us to hold dear. Further, when one begins to take into account major generational shifts even in "Anglo" culture (Boomers, Busters, Twenty-somethings, retirees, etc.) the compartmentalization of society stretches the limits so far as to produce a profound balkanization, fragmentation, and atomization of American society. Eventually, "ethnicity" is reduced to the peculiarities of each individual person. That would mean taking the HUP to its absurd extreme of encouraging the creation of a church for every person. But maybe this is not so extreme as we think, given the present North American context.[59]

Van Engen has another problem with the HUP—what does it say about the universality of the Gospel?

Whether intended or not on the part of McGavran, Wagner, Arn and others in the American Church Growth Movement, the emphasis on homogeneous units tends to stress cultural differences to such a degree that oneness, togetherness, the universality of the Gospel is in danger of being lost. ... I mean to point here too the fact that too strong an emphasis on the HUP makes its strengths (cultural sensitivity, contextualization, receptor-oriented communication, careful targeting, and wise presentation of the Gospel in appropriate ways for specific audiences)–become glaring weaknesses. They too quickly can atomize social cohesion and relegate persons to ever smaller units of homogeneity–completely ignoring the ways in which all persons share common human traits within a social structure which calls for common sharing of resources and experiences. In our present context in North America, especially in our cities, persons from so-called "homogeneous" groups may in fact represent people who all together attend the same schools, use the same banks, shop in the same stores, go to the same health facilities, use the same freeways, enjoy the same entertainments, rent the same videos, and maybe even live in the same neighborhoods. To divide these persons up into little "homogeneous units" is in fact to superimpose a social viewpoint that may be quite foreign to the reality of North America today.[60]

E. W. Hayward stated his objections to the HUP more sharply:

The homogeneous unit principle evades the challenge of the Gospel and of the Christian Church just where it becomes most real, most painful and most meaningful.[61]

And:

The crucial application of the Gospel to the Christian community was precisely the crossing of a racial barrier, and demonstration (which was not what either Jew or Gentiles liked) that in Christ, Jew and Gentile were made one.[62]

He's not done yet. He goes to the motive behind creating churches of homogeneous character:

It must be made clear that the Church of Jesus Christ stands for the overcoming, and not the perpetuation, of racial and class barriers. ... It does not matter if local congregations represent only one class or race because this is how they have naturally grown, provided the significance of the Church's universal nature is taught and understood; but it involves a betrayal of the Gospel and the Church if they are deliberately formed of one race, tribe, sub-tribe, cast or clan when the composition of their membership could have been broader, but was deliberately limited.[63]

Francis Duboce will go on to critique the Homogeneous Principle by calling for a Heterogeneous Principle.

Let us look at the homogenous unit concept in relation to urbanism. A serious problem in making this principle the normative strategy for church growth is that an urban society is heterogeneous in the normative expression of its public life. It is true that the homogenous groups exist in the private spheres and are therefore a legitimate expression of urban life. However, a strategy which is geared almost exclusively to homogeneity fails to recognize the significance of heterogeneity in urban society. ... People are constantly changing in the urban context, moving out of one identity into another and moving as a daily lifestyle in a cross-cultural and ever-changing social pattern. The public pressure of a massive changing and complex urban society is enormous. To get on this wavelength means we must develop a strategy for the 'heterogeneous principle'".[64]

Thus far, we've looked at three major concerns with the concept of the Homogeneous Unit Principle of church planting:

1. The HUP, knowingly or unknowingly, perpetuates and even justifies the segregation by race, ethnicity, class etc.

2. The homogenous principle has sometimes been presented as *the one* valid church principle for church growth regardless of context, rather than one of a number of tools a missionary might use to plant a church.

3. The HUP magnifies God's activity in the particular (locality) at the expense of God's universal activity. Over-commitment to the homogeneous principle may detract from the doctrine of the Oneness of Christ's Body, limiting the manifestation of diversity at a local level. The result is to undermine the universal characteristic of the Gospel.

Let's address the possible harm in an exaggerated valuation of the HUP. Discussing the role the HUP can play in maintaining unjust social systems, Michael Emerson and Christian Smith, in their important research-supported book *Divided by Faith*, note the following:

The organization of American religion into racially homogeneous groups lowers the probability of intergroup mobility (such as through marriage) and heightens the importance of racial boundaries, identities, and other differences between groups. Although many in the religious community call and work for an end to racial division, the organization of religion into homogeneous groups often undercuts their effort.[65]

Viewing the homogeneous principle as more than a tool elevates the concept beyond what it really is. First, the concept originates from observations of how society functions. As Wagner admits, it is sociological and not theological—its conclusions are useful only as they help spread the Gospel and grow the church. When that is not the case, we need to look at other tools for church planting.

What about the church of Acts 11:19–26? A multicultural approach proved effective in communicating the Gospel in multicultural Antioch.

When we consider how to communicate the gospel to recent immigrants this discussion moves out of the seminary classroom and encounters real life and real families. We cannot assume that the ministry approach that works for the first-generation Ethiopian immigrant group will also work for their children, Generations 1.5 and 2.0. They are like their parents only in regard to their DNA, their blood. The Generation 1.5 and 2.0 Ethiopians and Eritreans say they are more American than they are Ethiopian, or as least they are members of both cultures. They have assimilated into

American society. My research data shows their social and cultural identity resembles other urban Americans of their generation, who are not Ethiopian. Notice David Britt's comment on this challenge:

> What does homogeneity mean in the city? It may be that the ethical discussion over the homogeneous unit principle as a strategic ploy, as helpful and as necessary as this discussion has been, has side-tracked any fuller discussion of the actual dynamics of social groupings in urban contexts. Perhaps part of the problem is that word "homogeneity" connotes a thoroughgoing social consistency that is strange to urban memories. If we may bracket the question of oughtness for a moment, do I in fact go to church with my own kind of people? Is that possible? I am not entirely sure which kind my own kind of people would be. In fact, one of my chief blessings and frustration as an urbanite can be that I am not entirely sure which kind of person I really am; the answer most likely is that I am many kinds of people at once, depending on the circle with whom I interact at any given moment.[66]

Yes, Generation 1.5 and 2.0 generation Ethiopians belong ethnically to the Ethiopian/Eritrean community but culturally they more closely resemble other Americans of their generation than they do their own parents. Therefore, ministry to the 1.5 and 2.0 generations cannot be like that to their parents.

Let us now turn to the theology of planting a church. What message about God and His Kingdom do our church planting methods tell the world?

Once the Jew/Gentile controversy took center stage, as the church made huge inroads into Gentile communities, it was the Apostle Paul—both as a missionary and a thinker—who addressed the challenges of culture, religious background and ethnicity. Paul was a Jew, born and raised outside Palestine, in Tarsus. Although Jewish, he possessed Roman citizenship (Acts 22:27f) and he was steeped in both Jewish and Greek cultures. This combination of experience and spirit enabled him to preach Jesus Christ as the bridge between sinners and a loving God and also as the bridge between Gentiles and Jews. Writing to the Ephesians in Ephesians 2:11–18 he describes the Berlin Wall that existed between Jews and Gentiles in his day and God's decisive action to dismantle that wall forever in Jesus Christ.

> [11] Therefore, remember that formerly you who are Gentiles by birth and called "uncircumcised" by those who call themselves "the circumcision" (that done in the body by the hands of men)— [12] remember that at that time you were separate from Christ, excluded from citizenship in Israel and foreigners to the covenants of the promise, without hope and without God in the world. [13] But now in Christ Jesus you who once were far away have been brought near through the blood of Christ. [14] For he

himself is our peace, who has made the two one and has destroyed the barrier, the dividing wall of hostility, [15] by abolishing in his flesh the law with its commandments and regulations. His purpose was to create in himself one new man out of the two, thus making peace, [16] and in this one body to reconcile both of them to God through the cross, by which he put to death their hostility. [17] He came and preached peace to you who were far away and peace to those who were near. [18] For through him we both have access to the Father by one Spirit. [19] Consequently, you are no longer foreigners and aliens, but fellow citizens with God's people and members of God's household, [20] built on the foundation of the apostles and prophets, with Christ Jesus himself as the chief cornerstone. [21] In him the whole building is joined together and rises to become a holy temple in the Lord. [22] And in him you too are being built together to become a dwelling in which God lives by his Spirit. (Ephesians 2:11–18)

In verses 11–13 Paul reminds Gentiles that in prior times they were excluded from citizenship in Israel, with no covenant promise, no hope and without God in this world. But things were different now. Because of Jesus' sacrifice on the cross for them, and His shed blood, they have been brought in, reconciled first with Him, and included now among the people of God.

The implications of God's action (Ephesians 2:4–22) boggles the mind. Through Jesus Christ, God has reconciled both Jews and Gentiles to himself. Barriers and walls tumble. In fact, out of the despised Jews and the disgusting Gentiles, God has determined to create one new man or one new people. F. F. Bruce in his commentary on Ephesians writes:

> Whereas Jews formerly tended to speak of the division of humanity into Jews and Gentiles, Paul makes a threefold classification into Jews, Greeks (Gentiles), and church of God (1 Cor. 10:32), the last embracing former Jews and former Gentiles. No wonder that Christians spoke of themselves as a "third race" or "new race," no longer Jewish, no longer Gentile. The barrier which formerly separated Jews and gentiles has been demolished in Christ. This traditional barrier was both religious and sociological.[67]

God has created one new people, who all have access to God and who now experience peace among themselves, regardless of their backgrounds. In fact, Paul says (Ephesians 2:19–22), they are now one family, "members of God's household." Because they have one Father who indwells them all through his Spirit, they have become sisters and brothers! What a beautiful picture of the new community of Christ! It was the *tour de force* of Paul's teaching, his master stroke that he would present wherever he preached and planted churches. Did Paul and his team focus on planting homogeneous churches and avoid multicultural ministry? Not a word of it!

Van Engen, in describing the universal characteristic of the Church, comments in his discussion on Ephesians 2:11–22:

> Because it is for all people, the church may never cease to call, to invite, to draw everyone to him. The Church catholic rightly belongs in the highways and byways as the messenger carrying a special invitation. The Church catholic is a completely open fellowship, with its doors always spread wide, open to all. The Church catholic cannot diminish its universality by exclusivism, be it social, economic, racial, sexual, cultural, or national. The Church catholic is by its very nature missionary, sent to all people precisely because the Head of the Church "fills all in all."[68]

Yes, American society is gerrymandered into racial, ethnic, cultural and social grouplets. Powerful political and economic traditions and laws and structures build up the walls of this system. Yes, it may be the reality we experience daily, but as Christians we cannot dismiss the fact that an exaggerated view of the Homogeneous Unit Principle, whether intentionally or unintentionally, maintains the segmentation of the Christian church and undermines its universal characteristic—a danger that Christians cannot afford to view lightly. Christians, being part of the culture, are vulnerable to accepting society's norms uncritically. We often lack eyes to critically see that which undermines our own core beliefs.

At this point I'd like to use an example, to show how an ethnocentric attitude can undermine the universality of the church. Let's look at how religious faith relates to nationalism. Donald Fairbairn devotes a chapter of his book in his book on the Eastern Orthodox Church to "Orthodoxy and Nationalism." He offers the following definition for religious nationalism:

> Religious nationalism is essentially a confusion of people's religious sensibilities with their nationalistic interest, and it manifests itself in the belief that a particular nation or ethnic group, as a whole, is closer to God than other nations (or, in extreme form, the belief that one's own nation alone is the beneficiary of God's favor). This belief frequently leads people to make ironclad distinctions between their own nation as "good" and others as "evil" and renders them unable to distinguish between religious and nationalistic concerns.[69]

As Fairbairn traces the history of religious nationalism, he points out that "during the Western Middle Ages and the Byzantine period in the East, nationalism was (to some degree) held in check by the larger political and social units."[70] Eastern Christians saw themselves as part of the Byzantine

Empire (which included people of different ethnicities and national identities). Similarly, the Holy Roman Empire served to give the Church in the West a larger identity than one based on ethnic or national identity. However, as these larger political systems fell apart in the late Middle Ages, the social structures attached themselves to the developing nation states, ushering in the rise of religious nationalism.[71]

After the Eastern Church and Western Church split in 1054, forming the churches we now call the Eastern Orthodox and the Roman Catholic Churches, the two churches developed divergent histories, down into the Twenty-first Century. Nationalism in the West tied closely with the Age of Exploration, Conquest and Colonialism. Religious nationalism often drove these efforts along. Roman Catholic explorers and kings and queens in Spain and Portugal Christianized their subjects far from their homeland, as did Protestant explorers from the Netherlands, England and later the United States, expanding their power in the world with their brand of Christianity (Anglican, Dutch Reformed, etc.).[72] In the East, when the cohesive power of the Empire collapsed, the different national churches also emerged. Fairbairn tells the story of the Eastern Empire's disintegration into national churches.

> This alliance was not nationalistic, because the empire was seen as a universal one that incorporated many groups of people within the fold of Christian Hellenism. However, as the empire eroded during

Middle Ages, ... The idea thus changed into one of Greek nationalism and the desire to preserve the Greek nature of the Church, rather than the universal church of the earlier period. ... At the same time, the other Eastern Churches that had begun as part of the Byzantine Empire (particularly Serbia, Bulgaria, and Russia) began to assert their independence from Constantinople and to understand their heritage as Slavic, rather than simply Byzantine. The fact that they had been encouraged from the beginning to use their own languages, rather than Greek for worship and preaching contributed to this sense of nationalism. ... In this atmosphere, the idea began to arise in the East that each nation stands before God on its own.[73]

While the Western Church was on it course of expansion into new territories, the Church in the East was fighting against Islam for self and national preservation. The organization of the two churches also made a difference. Fairbairn states, "Unlike Roman Catholicism, which is organized into a hierarchy whose locus of power and authority is centralized, the Chalcedonian Orthodox Churches"[74] and non-Chalcedonian churches are organized into local bodies. He adds, "the belief frequently arises that the nation or ethnic group stands in a special relationship to God. This organizational structure has historically made Orthodoxy somewhat more prone to the development of nationalism than Roman Catholicism."[75]

Although Catholic and Protestant nations are vulnerable to religious nationalism, the degree of religious nationalism in Eastern Orthodox Churches—both Chalcedonian and so-called non-Chalcedonian—appears greater. Roman Catholicism's international and hierarchical system projects the universal character of the Church, while the Protestant denominational construct found in many parts of the world—regardless of its country of origin—also may project an international face, although less than that of the Roman Catholic Church.

> Fairbairn calls religious nationalism out as heresy:
> Religious nationalism is not the product of official Orthodox doctrine regarding the Church. Lossky asserts that in the face of Catholicity, the wholeness of the Church, the very notion of a national church is erroneous. Meyendorff calls religious nationalism "the bane of modern Orthodoxy," and Schmemann is even more direct when he asserts that religious nationalism is essentially a heresy about the Church, since it views people as divided into "one's own" and "the aliens" and prevents catholicity... The Church is a gathered community of the faithful in a single place for the purpose of reflecting the future age when division and imperfection will be overcome, when all creation will be united to God. Because of this community, any national divisions (or, for that

matter, any division at all) are inappropriate within the Church.[76]

Religious nationalism leads to terrible consequences, he says:

> Zernov and Meyendorff both comment on the tragic results of nationalism within Orthodoxy. Zernov writes that in the last five hundred years the church has been so closely associated with nationalism that people have confined Orthodoxy to their own ethnic group and become indifferent to the religious condition of the rest of the world. Meyndorff asserts, "Instead of the Church making a legitimate use of cultural pluralism in order to make its message heard and better understood, the various nationalisms are making use of the Church in order to achieve their own goals." These national commitments... "constitute real cover for *de facto* separatism. They inhibit the missionary spirit and hide the universal nature of the Church."[77]

I took this detour through the Eastern Orthodox Church and its nationalistic characteristic to highlight the danger of dividing the Church on the basis of geography, language or culture. Homogeneity can be a useful tool. However, ignoring the universal character of the Church in local and international expressions opens up the danger of falling into extreme particularity, which contradicts the universal nature of the Church.

We've looked at how multicultural congregations played a key role in the history of the early church (Book of Acts). Such churches must be encouraged to develop in North America today. Yet unquestioned commitment to 'multicultural' creates the opposite problem. The particularity of the local church can be undermined. So, the call goes forth for balance and contextualization on the local level, while we seek the universal character of the Church on the national and international level.

1.5 and 2.0 Ethiopians and Multicultural Church Models

According to my data findings, Generation 1.5 and 2.0 Ethiopians identify themselves as bicultural and may prefer Christian ministry that is multicultural. DeYoung, Emerson, Yancey and Kim, in their ground-breaking study on multicultural congregations titled *United by Faith,* sample and analyze multicultural churches.

> During the course of our research, we came across many different types of multicultural congregations. In some, we found that there is definitely one dominant racial group in terms of leadership or congregational culture. Members of the congregation who were not part of the dominant racial group simply adapted to the existing congregational culture. In other congregations, we observed elements of several different cultures incorporated into the worship services, and we also noted a more racially integrated leadership. These congregations

had arrived at their state only after struggling to respond to the voices of increasingly diverse membership. In still other congregations, we noted that the relationship could not necessarily be characterized by racial integration; it was more a state of coexistence. The different racial groups may sit together in the pews, but the informal social networks within the congregations are racially separate. ... These observations led us to create the following three ideal-type categories to describe the overall congregational culture and the degree of racial integration. 1) Assimilated multicultural congregation; 2) Pluralist multicultural congregation; and 3) Integrated multicultural congregation.[78]

The authors then detail these three types. They describe the 'Assimilated Multicultural Congregation' as follows:

In the assimilated model, one racial group is obviously the dominant group within the congregation. This group's dominance is reflected in the worship services activities, and leadership. Congregation members who do not belong to the dominant racial group simply "assimilate" into the existing culture. In other words, the way a congregation functions is not significantly changed by the presence of the members from different groups.[79]

Most assimilated multiracial churches were born as mono-racial churches and, as the congregation demographics changed, they became multiracial. Despite this change, the possibility of prioritizing the original racial culture remains. And churches that were initially multiracial could end up as this type, as an assimilated multiracial congregation, if one race or one group's culture continues to dominate the church culture.

The second ideal-type multicultural church model is the "Pluralist Multiracial Congregation." The authors describe how this church type functions:

> The second type of congregation that we found is the pluralist multiracial congregation. In this type of congregation, physical integration has occurred, in the sense that members of different racial groups choose to gather in the same church and worship service. They are all members of the same congregation. Although this physical integration is notable, members do not move beyond coexistence to real integration of social networks. While official committees may be multicultural, the informal social networks still remain segregated by race.[80]

This model describes a single congregation with several racial or ethnic groups in it. In this kind of pluralistic church model, leaders strive to balance the congregation by making sure each group gets representation and visibility. In such a system, groups are encouraged to maintain their own cultures, which makes it difficult for a member to reach across the aisle to someone from another group.

The third church model is the "Integrated Multicultural Congregation."

> Integrated Multicultural Congregation is to us the theological ideal, but it is also the rarest of the three. It is our belief that a truly multicultural congregation requires a transformation of congregational culture. It is no longer the old culture with certain accommodations made for members of different races, and it is no longer a mosaic with elements of separate and distinct cultures. Rather, the integrated multiracial congregation has developed a hybrid of distinct cultures that have joined together in one church. Elements of distinct cultures are not incorporated to "appease" diverse constituencies; rather, the new hybrid culture is an expression of the congregation's unified collective identity. The relationship among members of different races in the congregation are strictly egalitarian.[81]

Although the authors tout this approach as best for Generation 1.5 and 2.0 immigrants, achieving such a congregation requires deliberate thought and strategy. Where large numbers of Ethiopian immigrants live, in cities such as Washington DC and Los Angeles, planting a daughter Generation 1.5 and 2.0 church from a single Ethiopian immigrant church is possible. However, this only represents the starting place. In order to become an integrated multicultural church, leaders need to reach out to other 1.5 and 2.0 generation immigrants who are not Ethiopians. They also need to reach out to American Millennials.

Overflow Church in Silver Spring, MD is a shining example (See Section III of this book for the Overflow Story). In other major U.S. cities, other church plants look to Overflow as a model. These churches are 90%+ Ethiopian and Eritrean, so how do they build bridges to other immigrant communities and to the American millennials?

Where the Ethiopian population is small and the churches are small, with few Generation 1.5 and 2.0 folks, we should look at church planting partnerships. Churches who partner together can be Ethiopian, non-Ethiopian recent immigrants and American groups. We use the "social capital theory"— the concept that social relationships are resources that can be developed. We start with a community of multiple cultures and work towards the creation of an integrated multicultural experience. Right now, I label this approach 'theoretical' because we don't see any congregations in the Ethiopian community where this is happening successfully.

Naysayers and skeptics will, of course, raise their voices when we talk about collaboration and partnerships. However, this concept is not far-fetched. People may come from different levels of conviction as they look to plant a multicultural church. Many, like Ken Uyeda Fong, will start with the immediate need to start an ethnic English-speaking church and find themselves attracting a pan-ethnic group, and, to their astonishment, break even that mold and become a church that truly reflects the American mosaic. Consider Fong's story, the story of a pastor of a multicultural church in Southern California, which he describes in his book, *Pursuing the Pearl*:

> When I first answered the call to pastoral ministry in 1977, I thought that the Lord was directing me to pastor only English-speaking Chinese Americans. Three years later, when I relocated to Southern California to complete my degree at Fuller Seminary, God amended my understanding to include English-speaking Japanese Americans. Nine years after my first call, the Lord again amended my understanding, this time to include English-speaking Korean Americans. Not long after that, I concluded that my original interpretation had been too narrow, that all along God had called me to pastor English-speaking Americanized Asian Americans.[82]

> He adds:
> While it is true that a high percentage of Asian Americans live within a fifteen-mile radius, our immediate neighbors tend to be mid-to-lower income Latino Americans and White Americans. As we began reaching out to them with various ministries, it got to the point where it was too awkward saying that this was an exclusive multi-Asian church. Thus, in 1997 we opened the gates to all our neighbors

by adding multi-ethnic to our vision statement. ...
As the non-Asian American portion of our body
continuous to grow, we realize that we will be able
to come together as a kingdom community...[83]

SEVEN

25 Young Ethiopians Speak

I arrived at Concordia Seminary in Ft. Wayne, Indiana in 2003 with one burning issue on my mind:

How can we reach our children who are drifting down the cultural river of America and already look almost out of sight?

However, this was not my professor's burning issue. As a leader in the Lutheran Church, he was looking at dying churches around the U.S., especially in the big cities. The populations of neighborhoods around urban Lutheran churches were shifting. Church attendance had fallen dramatically, in many congregations, to a handful of older white folks who had moved to the suburbs. They commuted, now, to their inner-city churches, which were surrounded by black and brown communities who did not attend Lutheran churches. How about that for a research topic?

This did not answer the question that had motivated me to relocate two thousand miles from San Jose to Indiana. Fortunately, my wife Abby is a fighter. She encouraged me to stand firm. Yes, the Professor's topic was an important one but 'you came here for another reason,' she reminded me. And over a period of time, I persuaded the Professor to permit me to research my issue:

What are the immigrant children, the 1.5 and 2.0 generations, really like and how can we build Christian ministries to reach and retain them?

After landing on the focus, my next step was devising a survey to answer these questions. I would recruit twenty-five Ethiopian-American, Eritrean-American young people. But not just any twenty-five. I had to set boundaries and select my targets very carefully. I developed the following criteria:

One. You must be the child of an Ethiopian immigrant to the U.S., at least eighteen years old today, and able to reflect on your experience of growing up.

Two. You will either be a Generation 2.0, meaning your parents immigrated to the U.S. and you were born here, or a Generation 1.5, which means you were born in the Old Country, experienced a bit of Ethiopia, even some schooling, but you immigrated before the age of twelve.

Three. Your family is Christian, either Protestant or Orthodox, but your present status regarding your Christian upbringing will not influence whether I include you or not.

Four. We will conduct the interview in English, so you need to be able to communicate your experiences to me in English.

I knew a lot of immigrant Ethiopians, so finding twenty-five who fit these criteria didn't seem insurmountable. In fact, I could start with several young people in the congregation I had been pastoring in San Jose. I began there and recruited eight candidates in Northern California. My doctoral advisor, Professor Rutt, and I agreed the survey would be most valuable if it represented the larger nation and I proceeded to look for recruits in other major cities. When I discovered Ethiopian college students held a nationwide celebration annually and that year Washington, DC was hosting it, I flew there and met a number of candidates.

I had hoped to survey both Protestant and Orthodox families/churches—which faith group was more successful in keeping their young people? Right away I encountered problems with this idea. Before my trip to Washington, I met with the head priest of a Bay Area Orthodox church. He listened attentively and promised to take my request for interview candidates to his board, but his board turned me down. They didn't trust me. I was quite disappointed. On the trip to D.C. I deliberately sought out Orthodox students. Although several gave me their names and email addresses, when I contacted them after the trip, most did not return my emails. *Then I caught a lucky break.* A friend who lived in Fresno heard about my project and offered to introduce me to four or five Orthodox young men who lived in that city. I drove over and successfully recruited several. My sample of Orthodox young people remained too small, however, to make a thorough comparison of Orthodox and Protestant immigrant children.

I then developed a set of interview points to answer my Big Question:

1. Describe your experience in America and how you identify yourself today.
2. Describe how the Host Society (meaning the American culture, in most places equal to White America) has shaped your identity.
3. Describe how your Ethnic Community (meaning the Ethiopian culture of your family, your church, and any friends) has shaped who you are today.
4. Describe how your experience as a Christian or your childhood in a Christian family has shaped you.

I purchased the best recording equipment I could find: an Olympus Digital Voice Recorder, which boasted superior audio recording quality. Because it records digitally, the resulting files can be uploaded onto a computer and then turned into an English transcript, using a Sony digital voice editor and software. I also recruited my son, Daniel, and offered him the going minimum wage of eight dollars an hour to edit the interview recordings for me, using a headset and foot control machine. Voice editors were very approximate in 2008 and even with artificial intelligence software today, the editor spits out sentences that often contain unrecognizable words or very bad guesses. Transcription takes many hours of methodical attention to detail, yet Daniel was willing—by the end of the project he would transcribe five hundred single spaced pages of the interviews.

I set to work calling interview candidates and making appointments. Of the twenty-five candidates I recruited, ten were women, fifteen men. Seven were born in the U.S. and therefore represented Generation 2.0; eighteen were born in Ethiopia and were therefore Generation 1.5. At the time of my interviews in 2008–09, fifteen were aged eighteen to twenty-four, ten were twenty-five to thirty-three. Only five had ever returned to Ethiopia. Four were already parents, and of the four, three were single parents who had partnered with a non-Ethiopian to bring a child into the world.

As much as possible, I did the interviews in person, flying to Denver and D.C. and driving to Sacramento and Fresno. I met most of the candidates at their home churches, where we sat across from each other and I presented my questions, as the recording machine ran on. Telling the stories of their journeys into American culture often brought up strong emotions for them. The interviewees told stories of being misunderstood from multiple sides—their families, their school mates, teachers ...

A young Ethiopian-American in D.C. cried as she described her youth. They were below the poverty line immigrants when they arrived, and her father took a position as a priest in an Orthodox church in Washington. She recounted how his new church had not appreciated him. "He sacrificed so much for them, but they stabbed him in the back." She recalled her high school years in a private, wealthy high school where the students flaunted their wealth and sense of entitlement. When I asked if she felt at home in the U.S. now, she said no, and stated, "I wish I could move to another country. Not Ethiopia. Maybe Germany. Some place where nobody knows me."

A young man I interviewed in Sacramento came from a family of three brothers who immigrated here in his childhood. His older brother failed to adjust and ended up in prison, where he is still incarcerated. The second brother achieved extraordinary success and went to Stanford on scholarship. He himself had felt alone and abandoned as a child. "I will never go to an Ethiopian church," he said.

My goal with the interviews was to listen to their stories and translate the findings into knowledge I could act on. Although the individual stories were sometimes heart-rending, my goal was to discover: What did all the participants experience as they journeyed from life as an Ethiopian child or the child of immigrant Ethiopians through assimilation into American culture? What universal patterns had each of them experienced? As I pored over the transcripts Daniel was producing and graphed the results, I arrived at six patterns or themes that described experiences common to all of the interviewees. I listed up the themes and then grouped the stories around them as I wrote the thesis. (Please refer to the Glossary for definitions of these terms).

- Ethiopian-ness
- Fitting In
- Blackness
- American-ness
- In-Between and In-Both
- Spirituality

When I finished the dissertation, I prepared to defend my conclusions.

The Defense was set for a snowy day in Ft. Wayne and the whole school had been invited to the Defense, as was customary at Concordia. I sent the Committee—my advisor, Dr. Douglas Rutt and the two thesis readers, Dr. Eric Moeller and Dr. Bob Newton—the full thesis some time beforehand but for most of the attending faculty and students, it was their first time to hear the results of my two-year journey. The defense lasted somewhere between three and four hours and at the end the listeners applauded, graciously, but I sensed politeness, some holding back. It seemed to me from their questions and pleasant applause that the professors, all of them Lutheran and Caucasian, were wondering: How important is this topic for the Church in North America, anyway? Is it really that urgent?

In any case, the Committee approved the thesis and I have their signatures, dated February 13, 2009, approving the dissertation in partial fulfilment of the requirements for my degree of Doctor of Philosophy in Missiology!

Regardless of what anyone else at the Seminary thought, the conclusions were fuel for me. They felt as urgent as the headlines of the morning paper. I had written something that I wanted every Ethiopian mother and father, every pastor in every small Ethiopian congregation across the U.S.A. to hear. Would the Ethiopian immigrant parent and the immigrant pastor appreciate what I had to say? Or would they say like the Concordia professors: Interesting, but is it important?

I want to say to them: I'm hopeful! Your children are not first of all victims of American racism, or generation gap, or any other crippling social malady. They will bring the gospel of Jesus Christ to this country. They are equipped to do that because they are bicultural. The passion of the Global South, where the Church of Jesus Christ is growing like crazy, flows through their veins as they walk the streets of the North, where faith has grown cold and small in many places where churches are dying. Your children trade with the values of two cultures because, among the most successful immigrant children, they are truly bicultural, something I will never be to the degree that they are. Their ability to live simultaneously with two identities is a mighty weapon in the arsenal of the Church of Jesus.

THEME ONE: Ethiopian-ness

As I began my interviews, I found that all twenty-five participants self-identified with pride as Ethiopians. They each described some piece of the culture that they loved. This became even more true for the older interviewees. As they spoke about their parents and Ethiopian people, they expressed positive feelings overall. However, the interviewees also talked frankly about negative aspects of their ethnicity, culture, and the challenge of relating to their first-generation parents and the first-generation immigrant community. We could characterize their outlook as a "love and hate" relationship with their Ethiopian-ness.

A number of patterns caught my attention. First, my participants always spoke of their ethnicity with a bicultural label. 'I am not only Ethiopian; I am also an American.' While Gen 1.5 interviewees used words like: I am culturally American but Ethiopian by heritage, Gen 2.0 interviewees saw themselves as Americans by birth. Yet both groups labelled themselves 'Ethiopian American.' Another pattern was a growing appreciation for their ethnicity as the participants grew older—when they were younger, a majority had wanted to distance themselves from their ethnicity. Still another pattern was the difference between Gen 1.5 and Gen 2.0 young people in the ability and desire to relate and identify with their parents' generation. The Gen 1.5 group felt culturally and emotionally equipped to maintain relationships with the first-generation parents and community leaders, in contrast with those who had been born here in America. However, the second-generation participants appeared better equipped and more willing to engage with American culture than those interviewees who had come here in their elementary school days.

Self-identification of Interviewees

Identify Biculturally **92%**

Identify only ethnically **8%**

But here's an irony! There is no ethnic group in Africa called 'Ethiopian'! Ethiopian-ness is only a national identity, the name on your passport. Why is that? Because Ethiopia as a nation is composed of multiple ethnic groups. A person is an Amhara or an Oromo or a Tigre or a Gurage. This makes complete sense to Gen 1, the generation of the parents. However, their children in the U.S. didn't usually take account of these ethnic tribal differences. Perhaps they were not aware of them, growing up in this country, or perhaps identifying as an ethnic group member didn't interest them.

One American born interviewee said, "I identify with Ethiopians. When I go home, I see Ethiopian parents, family and their friends. I have a lot in common with them. I feel comfortable with them in a way that I don't with other people, but I do not think that is my entire identity ..."

A second interviewee, who was two and half years old when he and his parents immigrated to this country, described his ethnic identity as, "I will say I am Ethiopian American; Ethiopian by heritage and American by culture and nation." The language skill of this young man at the time of his parents' arrival was minimal; he said today he had very limited Amharic vocabulary and no memory of Ethiopia. He grew up in an American city with a very small Ethiopian population. Other than his family, he didn't socialize with any other Ethiopians. He was the first and only child when the family arrived, which meant his childhood friends were all out-group kids.

With the help of television and the out-group, his non-Ethiopian neighborhood friends, he picked up English before he knew the ethnic language well. Before starting first grade, he had mastered English and the American culture. In school, he quickly fit in and then joined the school's basketball team, a sport he continued through high school. His skills on the basketball court won him acceptance in the African American group in high school. Although his parents devoted time to the Ethiopian church, due to his association with the African American community through sports he had little time for the Ethiopian community. As a result, he never learned Amharic, and his primary relationships today are with Americans and not Ethiopians. In adolescence, he made a profession of faith in Jesus through the ministry of an English-speaking church. At the time of his interview with me, he had risen to a leadership position in that church. Today, he identifies more with the American church, although the Ethiopian population in the city where he lives has increased and there is an Ethiopian congregation in the city.

One young woman said, "I am proud of my people and my culture…. It makes me happy to be an Ethiopian. I tell people I am Ethiopian and *only* Ethiopian. I am so proud of my culture." Her face positively glowed as she expressed her affection for her people and community. Growing up as a Gen 1.5 generation immigrant, arriving here at age twelve, she had not been proud of her ethnic group. She freely discussed her difficult acculturation experience at home, school, and with fellow Ethiopian immigrants. She talked so much about wanting to be an American that it created problems for her at home. However, her views on Ethiopians and especially those from her Orthodox Church changed dramatically after a family tragedy. Her older brother died unexpectedly and the support she and her family received and continue to receive from the Ethiopian community after his death communicated much love to her. Most people in American society are not supportive, she believes, because Americans value community less and either don't know how or perhaps are unwilling to face tragic circumstances such as her family went through.

While I was getting a feel for the interviews, I felt a need to further define the questions. I developed four additional questions to further help my interviewees describe their self-identity.

1. Describe who you are ethnically.
2. Describe your relationship with the Ethiopian community.
3. Describe your relationship with the host culture (American non-immigrant community)
4. Who would you consider for marriage, when that time arrives?

I began exploring the second question next. What about their relationship with the Ethiopian community in America?

One American-born young man stated, "I don't feel comfortable in an all-Ethiopian setting." He attends an American church and says many of his best friends are out-group people although some of his friends are second-generation children of recent immigrants, like himself. His lack of Amharic language skills and cultural incompetence contribute to his sense of discomfort. He grew up in a city with a fair-sized Ethiopian community and an ethnic church, as well. His brothers were both Gen 1.5, immigrating at age eleven and eight. Both brothers spoke only the ethnic language on their arrival. Furthermore, his grandmother, who spoke only Amharic, practically raised him while his parents worked. Nevertheless, despite growing up with a first-generation extended family in a heavily ethnic home environment, this young man doesn't speak Amharic and prefers to hang out in American settings, rather than ethnic settings.

More than a third of the twenty-five participants said they felt misunderstood or not fully accepted by their parents, the first-generation population. However, most asked me not to quote them on this. Did they not want to say negative things about their culture which might get back to their parents? Did they feel this was just their own subjective experience? Or did they feel confused about the gap between them and their parents—perhaps it was simply a natural, generational gap?

Another interviewee expressed his sense of not belonging. "I do not feel accepted by the people [Ethiopians in America]. I do not have a strong sense of belonging to the ethnic group." This man immigrated to the U.S. at age eight and has retained moderate Amharic language skills. However, he says the ethnic community is judgmental, gossipy and overly conservative in their views. During our interview, he described his social world as people from the out-group and no meaningful connection with the Ethiopian community outside of his immediate family. A second young man, born in this country, said, "Ethiopians who came to this country [first-generation immigrants] don't see us [those born in the U.S] as the same as them." People like himself, born in this country, are not considered fully Ethiopian, he said, and he claimed this was not just his opinion but others like him felt the same way.

Although Gen 1.5 and Gen 2.0 youth self-identified as Ethiopians and appeared proud of their ethnicity, many of them said the community didn't fully embrace them. According to my readings of the social literature on the immigrant experience, feelings of non-acceptance stem from cultural difference and incompetence in the ethnic culture. The most critical cultural incompetence, in the minds of my interviewees, was lack of skill in the ethnic language. This isn't surprising. Social literature shows a strong relationship between ethnicity and language. Orozco and Orozco, in their book *Children of Immigration*, say, "While on the surface language is about communication, it is also a marker of identity and an instrument of power."[84]

One of my interviewees stated, "I no longer speak the language fluently; the English language won out. . . . It has been very hard for me to maintain my Ethiopian-ness. I lost the language. It is very hard to maintain both; one almost always wins." This young man immigrated at age two and half. Although he spoke minimal Amharic as a toddler, his skill has decreased since then. Currently, the language he uses daily is English. Orozco and Orozco say, "In reality, very few people can be considered 'balanced' bilinguals. Most bilinguals are in fact dominant in one language."[85] He also connected his loss of the ethnic language with difficulty in maintaining his ethnicity (Ethiopian-ness). He told me that his connection to his ethnic group is limited to his family relationships and all other friendships are relationships with host culture (American) people.

Another interviewee, who immigrated at age five, gave this insight. "I spoke Amharic when I came, and I still do, but I do not read or write Amharic. On a scale of one to ten, with ten being fluency, I'm a six. I am not bothered by my loss of the Amharic language or the fact that I do not read and write. I would rather know English in America than Amharic. I am okay as long as I can have some conversation with people." Clearly, he feels skill in Amharic does not contribute to his success in the larger society. Its value is limited to the ethnic community and his country of origin. There is no direct incentive for him to retain the ethnic language because his future is in this country, not the Old Country.

Language Skills of Interviewees

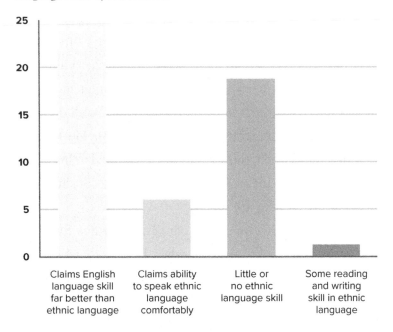

Finally, interviewees said ethnic identity issues led to conflict in their families. Nineteen of the twenty-five participants described conflict at home as they grew up. They characterized their parents (Gen 1.0) as overly strict. The conflicts surfaced around the issues of freedom, friendship, dating, cultural understanding, and so on. A young woman said:

> My mom is very Ethiopian, so she is very strict. She was afraid to let us play outside. Since other Ethiopians where we lived kept their kids in, she thought they knew something and would not let us

out. It was frustrating and we got into fights with my mom all the time. She was hard on all of us, including my brothers; but she was harder on me. Even after we moved to another neighborhood, she always worried and would try to keep us in and wouldn't like to let us play.... I didn't really get a chance to experience what was around me ... We had this apartment with a gate and my mom wouldn't let me pass the gate.... Whenever I compared my childhood with other kids, I wondered why my mom was so demanding and never gave me freedom and then I realized the difference in my parent's upbringing, compared to mine.... As we grew older, we didn't have time together as family. I would be out late and making my mom nervous. She would be mad with me, and I was angry too ... I wanted to be more American and never liked to talk to my family in Amharic.... My mom hated all of my friends. I always argued with my mother because I had a friend who was a good person in every sense except that she smoked cigarettes. My mother only focused on the fact that she smoked cigarettes; she didn't care about any of her personal qualities. My mom hated more than half of my friends.

This young woman's long description of her life growing up typifies the conflicts between the first-generation and the children (1.5 and 2.0) that I heard again and again in my interviews. The issue centered on control versus freedom. This may seem like the natural, generational conflict that exists in any culture. However, the interviewees believed the fears of their parents were driven by life in a strange and new society and culture. Gen 1.0 immigrants not only see themselves as outsiders, but to them, host culture (American) people and their practices are unusual and mysterious. In response, they become afraid and overprotective, which their children view as overly strict and controlling. This makes more sense when we consider how children are raised in the Ethiopian setting. Because Ethiopia is community-centric, relatives and neighbors, as well as parents, look after and correct children. Concerns about gangs and missing children are unheard of. When immigrant parents learn about such problems in the U.S., they react with fear. On the other hand, because they have grown up in American culture, children understand the host society better than their parents and the culture does not intimidate them. Parents attribute the comfort level of their children to the naiveté of youth. This misunderstanding on both sides complicates home life for both generations.

The misgivings that the children of immigrants feel about their ethnic identity are not limited to their relationships with their parents. My interview data shows that the 1.5s and 2.0s also harbored negative feelings toward America, the host culture, and the way it treated them. Nineteen out of twenty-five interviewees reported derogatory treatment and put-downs because of their ethnic identity. I conducted my interviews in 2008 and 2009, twenty-five years after the Ethiopian drought and famine of 1984–85. Many of the interviewees had grown up in the U.S., attending school here, and Ethiopia was prominent in the nightly news when they were in elementary or junior high.

One young woman told me her classmates would ask her, "How did you get so big? Who fed you? I heard everybody is dying over there." People would say, 'We saw you guys on TV.' People didn't think I was Ethiopian because I wasn't slim. Some said I was skinny with a bloated stomach. I didn't like that."

A young man reported that schoolkids called him by the name of a TV character. "On the TV show *South Park,* the character Starving Marvin is an Ethiopian; I have been called that a lot of times." One of my interviewees was told by her classmates, 'You are lucky that you are here,' as they talked about the famine. Another one stated, 'The Ethiopian stigma was stronger than the stigma of being called black.'

My Ethiopian-American interviewees also reported their non-Anglo-Saxon names caused problems. Since most of the 1.5 and 2.0's did not have a problem with accent, it was their names that triggered questions.

"My ethnicity would come out because of my name. It would start conversations." Other interviewees found their names a problem when it came to job interviews. Persons with 'American names' had greater success in receiving a call for a job interview. One woman stated:

On your work application, you will be passed if you do not have a regular American white name. They do not feel comfortable calling your name, which may be difficult for them to pronounce, and make them look ignorant.

The name could be a two-edged sword. Some immigrant children saw it creating an opportunity. "Whenever I get the opportunity, I will tell them [white Americans] I am from Ethiopia. The conversation may come up because of my name." She took advantage of people's curiosity about her name to highlight the fact that she was not a local African American. Another interviewee said, "My physical features and name were the way people identified me as an Ethiopian and not an African American'

Like many other immigrants to the U.S., some dealt with name problems by giving themselves Anglo-Saxon nicknames. They were following the path laid down by Kirk Douglas, born the Eastern Jewish boy, *Issur Danielovitch*; Rita Hayworth, the love goddess, who was born Margarita Carmen Casino; and Dean Martin, born Dino Crocetti.

Intermarriage serves as an indicator of how far a person has assimilated.[86] At the time of our interviews, twenty-three members of my survey had not yet married, so this provided an opportunity to probe them on their marriage partner criteria. Fifteen said they would prefer to marry within the Ethiopian-American community. Out of this group, only seven of the fifteen said marrying an in-group member was an absolute requirement.

Several said they were making their choice for the in-group in consideration of parents and the children. One young man said, "Although I feel comfortable with all women, despite ethnicity, my preference for marriage will be Ethiopian. It is better culturally and for my parents." Two women said they had considered marrying out-group when they were younger but had changed their minds, believing marriage with someone from the same culture made it easier for parents and children.

> Regarding marriage, I used to say, until age 15, I won't marry an Ethiopian. But then I started to see the difference in culture between the two worlds. Marrying someone from my culture, the families will unite, and it is smoother; so, I have shifted to prefer marrying an Ethiopian over an American.

Religion also complicates the choice of a marriage partner. Marriage to a spiritually compatible person raised the possibility of out-group marriage. Fifteen of the twenty-three still unmarried participants said religion was a more important consideration than ethnicity. The fifteen were all Protestants. Among the nine who did not view religion as an important consideration two were Protestants, five were Orthodox, one was Catholic, and one was atheist. Ironically, five of the fifteen who now stated that religion was more important than ethnicity had earlier in their interviews said marrying in-group was a must. They stated that they would marry an out-group person with a similar religious conviction over an Ethiopian or Ethiopian-American not of the same religious orientation.

In summary, sixteen of the twenty-three respondents indicated their openness to marrying an out-group person. However, when we add the five who strongly prefer to marry in-group but for religious reasons would consider marrying an out-group person, the number of interviewees open to marrying an out-group person grew to twenty–one of the twenty-three unmarried participants.

THEME TWO: Fitting In

The second question I pose in my thesis is: *How do 1.5 and second-generation Ethiopians in America describe the identity shaping impact of the host society (the U.S.)?* This question led me to sub-questions and surfaced three of the six patterns I discovered in my research.

The sub-questions below explore different aspects of the research question and helped me organize my survey answers to these questions under three themes. The sub-questions and the patterns I discovered were:

1. *How does the interviewee describe the challenge of being an immigrant in American schools? The pattern I found: Fitting In.*

2. *How do they describe being black in America? The pattern I found: Blackness.*

3. *How do they describe their experience of being an American? The pattern I found: American-ness.*

I'll look at each one of these questions and patterns in turn.

Fitting in

The term "fitting in" describes the challenge experienced by every one of the immigrant Ethiopian children in the American school setting. Interviewees told me that "fitting in" to their school environment presented far greater challenges than the education itself! This experience is not limited to Ethiopians—all immigrant families to the U.S experience it.

> Despite the Statue of Liberty's welcoming words:
> '*Give me your tired, your poor,*
> *Your huddled masses yearning to breathe free*'

The children of recent immigrants have all had to pass through this gauntlet.

Some factors that determine how severe this challenge will be include: How large is the number of ethnic kids in the school? How well known is the group in American society (think about the difference in reception between Chinese immigrant engineering families and Haitian boat people)? And how strong are their English language skills as they enter school?

Orozco and Orozco write:

Immigrant children typically come into contact with American culture sooner and, indeed more intensely, than their parents. Schools are an important site of cultural contact for immigrant children. It is where they meet teachers (who are often members of the dominant culture) as well as children from other backgrounds. For many immigrant children today, peers will be members of other ethnic and racial minorities. In schools they must contend quickly and intensively with the new culture.[87]

The data I collected from Gen 1.5 and Gen 2.0 immigrants agrees with the above statement. Thirteen of the twenty-five participants started kindergarten in this country, which means they did all of their schooling in host culture American schools. Four started in the elementary school—they had some schooling back in Ethiopia. Eight started middle school or junior high—they had a good amount of education prior to immigration.

School Experience

All schooling in America **62%**

Some schooling in Ethiopia **38%**

One young woman who immigrated at age twelve describes the experience of fitting into junior high and high school in a new country:

> I thought high school was going to be better because there were African Americans in the school. I thought I am African and maybe I will fit in better, but it was even harder because the African Americans basically looked at me as I am not black like them. So, I didn't fit in with African Americans; I didn't fit in with Caucasians and Mexicans; and I didn't fit in anywhere. So, high school was hard too. Sometimes I would fit in with mixed people—half white and half black because I resembled them more than African American or Caucasian persons. So, my only friends were half white and half black and some Mexicans here and there.

This young woman and her family had located in a large southwestern state where there were no Ethiopians in the school.

The young people I interviewed used various strategies to deal with the experience of loneliness and isolation. In cities and schools where more co-ethnics were present, Gen 1.5s often sought out other co-ethnics as friends. Gen 2.0 young people, born in the U.S., usually did not seek out other ethnics, even though they knew some in the school or in the area. In cities where there were few or no Ethiopian-

Americans, the Gen 1.5 generation group sought out Gen 1.5 immigrants from non-Ethiopian backgrounds—think Chinese and Vietnamese—and hung out with them. Those born in this country, on the other hand, easily befriended Americans, black or white, depending on the racial mix of the school. Curiously, in communities where there was a large population of Ethiopian-Americans, the Gen 1.5 and Gen 2.0 groups hardly mixed with each other. The 1.5 group sought out ethnic kids from other cultures and the second-generation didn't. Members of the American-born group melded with American social groups.

Another coping strategy, used especially by boys, was sports participation. One young man told me, "In junior and high school, I purposely chose to go to an inner-city school because they had a good basketball team, although academically the school wasn't good. Basketball opened a lot of doors for me socially. It became a way for me to fit in."

Seventeen of the twenty-five interviewees reported language difficulty. Language is not the only acculturation[88] challenge that children of immigrants face, but it is major. Language is an ethnic marker with social and cultural consequences. This is especially true for young people in school, who will experience ridicule and rejection over their inability to speak English fluently. One girl who came to the country at the age of eleven told her story of extreme embarrassment and shame:

I knew one Ethiopian girl in a higher grade than I was. She would tell me what to say and stuff but she wasn't always there. The American students in my class would make me say bad words and then laugh at me and I would laugh with them since I didn't understand. I realized shortly that they were laughing at me. One day I understood one of the words because back home we use it too and it is a very bad word; and I broke down to the teacher and started crying and I explained it to the Ethiopian girl because she was the only Ethiopian girl in my school, and they took me out of the class and put me into independent study.

The sense of shame this girl experienced was profound. She was fortunate to have a teacher who cared enough to tutor her separately until she got over her shame and embarrassment.

A young man who immigrated at age twelve highlighted the challenge of different groups who speak the same English language differently. This confused him. He states:

Junior high is not the best place to blend, in contrast to high school. The biggest barrier was language. The biggest challenge was not being able to understand the aspect of the English language that is cultural. That is, each group speaks English a certain way; Hispanics speak it one way, African

Americans have their slang and Caucasians theirs. In Ethiopia we are familiar with British English, which has a different cultural aspect. So, coming to America and hearing these different expressions was confusing. I wondered: what are they talking about? Slang is not associated with Ethiopia, what is going on? Language was definitely a barrier that I struggled with. Because of that I didn't identify with any group except immigrants. As immigrants we may not understand each other's accent, but we understand we all have a hurdle that we have to overcome. We met at the ESL class.

Nevertheless, at the time of my interviews with them, all twenty-five of the Gen 1.5 and Gen 2.0 survey participants stated their English language skills were stronger than their mother tongue. They described themselves as more comfortable in the English language than the home language. For that reason, I conducted my interviews 100% in the English language.

THEME THREE: Blackness

Black skin creates an issue for immigrant Ethiopians. Most Ethiopians do not consciously think of race as a category. Back in Ethiopia people notice the ethnicity of a person— what people group do they belong to? —but not race. When they immigrate to the U.S., many first-generation Ethiopians and their immigrating children become aware of race as a category for the first time. The data shows that it may take a few years before the immigrant begins to internalize blackness.

Elizabeth Chacko, in her research book on young Ethiopian immigrants, stated, "Hailing from a country where the taxonomy of populations is based largely on linguistic, religious, and tribal affiliations, race is not of particular concern until they are confronted with the practice of racial classification and the outcomes of racial hierarchy in the host country."[89] Citing her own research she adds:

"Nevertheless, with longer residence in the United States, especially among 1.5-generation youth, perceptions of Blackness and African-ness developed. In the sample, more than 70 percent reported that they became more aware of race and phenotype over time, as this quotation indicates: 'During the first couple of years [after arriving in the United States], I considered myself only Ethiopian. Then I started thinking of myself as African. As time passed... I interacted more with [native] Blacks and other Americans. This country made me more aware of my race. I was Blacker than I thought I was!' (Moges, 1.5 generation)."[90]

My interviewees confirmed Chacko's finding. Half of my Gen 1.5 interviewees said they didn't know they were black until they came to the U.S. Their expressions contained an element of surprise about this unexpected and unwanted discovery.

Consider this statement by one young man who immigrated at age twelve:

> I didn't know I was black until we came here. I
> had an Italian friend in Ethiopia who spoke Amharic,
> I never thought of him being white and me black . . .
> I knew I was African but never thought black. It was
> maybe in sixth or seventh grade that I realized I was
> black. It slowly began to bother me, nothing that hit
> me, it was a process. I knew I was different.

A young woman who also immigrated around age twelve
stated a similar experience. When she thought of herself as
black, she thought it must be a negative. She attempted to
ignore the facts at first and didn't accept them until she was
in high school.

> I didn't think about being black in Ethiopia. It
> was when I came here that I noticed that my skin is
> different, my hair texture is different from the others.
> I thought of it as a negative. I ignored it at first, but
> it was in high school that I started separating myself.

However, despite the fact that Gen 1.5 and 2.0 Ethiopians
immigrants in the United States discover their racial identity
slowly and reluctantly, the majority of them told me they
identify today as blacks and they identify with the American
black community.

Several said black organizations on the college campus
had helped them. "I see value in being part of African
American organizations in school," one interviewee told

me. "I was helped by some professors in the engineering department who were blacks. I understand that I must prove myself. They are great people and I want to be part of that in the future. Appreciation for the struggle of America's black community is well understood." Another interviewee said, "I believe it is important to participate out of respect as well. We benefit from their struggle and hard work. It is one thing I do not do enough." A third respondent said the personal trauma of discrimination is an experience immigrant children, like himself, share with black Americans and it becomes a reason to identify with the black community. She said, "I am closer to blacks because of the color of my skin and because I have also experienced some discrimination. I do identify more with African Americans than other groups, such as whites, Hispanics or Asians."

This self-identification may involve taking on African American cultural values. One respondent said, "I identify with African Americans. I like their music." Another added, "I listen to Hip Hop and R & B. I am a musician myself. I make that kind of music. I hope to make a living off it someday."

Identification with African American Community

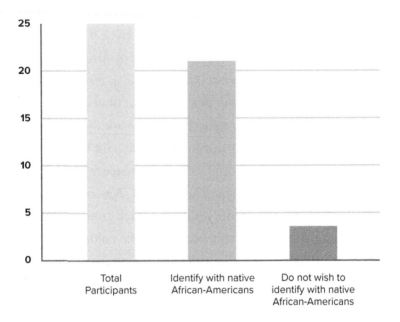

In addition to skin color, social mirroring and being labelled as 'black,' the experience of discrimination leads immigrant children from Ethiopia to self-identify with the U.S. African American population. More than two thirds of my interviewees said they had experienced direct personal discrimination.

One respondent stated his teacher accused him of cheating on a test because he did very well. He also said he was passed up for tutoring jobs in high school while his Asian friends got hired easily. The only difference, he believed, was his black skin. Several talked about discrimination in the workplace. They stated they were passed over for good job opportunities despite their performances, which compared favorably with white applicants. One young man said police officers harassed him in his middle-class neighborhood. In Texas, part of the historic South, the discrimination sometimes showed up even more raw and glaring. An interviewee who grew up in Dallas in the Eighties said:

"Our high school was a predominately white high school. We actually had Ku Klux Klan students in the school. In junior high, a big group of us blacks, with maybe a few Ethiopians, used to walk home from school together. KKK kids would sometimes chase us on foot or even chase us in their truck. There was a lot of indirect racism. If you walked into the cafeteria, it was completely segregated –and that amazed me when I considered how hard this country had fought for schools not to be like that—but if you walked into our school cafeteria it was pretty segregated."

Most of my interviewees stated their realization that they were going to be treated as blacks in this country, regardless of their origin as Ethiopians. They recognized that their future in this country was intertwined with the native African American community, and as a result, many of them saw how identifying with a larger population than their own specific ethnic group could bring benefits.

Despite this high self-identification with African Americans, Gen 1.5 and Gen 2.0 Ethiopians expressed ambivalence about their racial identity and their relationships with African Americans. This may be a result of negative encounters with the African American population. This relationship could be characterized as a love/hate relationship.

More than half of my interviewees recounted stories of rejection by members of the African American community. This confused and complicated their self-identification as black. One U.S. born respondent told me, "There is a weird identity divide between African Americans and Africans from the continent. I have been told 'You are not black; you are African or Ethiopian.' Yet other people would tell me 'We were all African, once upon a time.' A Gen 1.5 respondent said, 'When I was in high school, a fight broke out between African Americans and Africans. I don't remember the reason, but I thought: here we are, all of us black, and we are fighting against each other!'

Another thing that may complicate the relationship Ethiopian immigrant children have with African Americans is what I call 'First-generation Bias.' Several participants told me their first-generation immigrant parents pressured them to disassociate from African Americans. The issue is sensitive—the participants seemed uncomfortable talking about it. Perhaps they perceived it as betraying parental confidence. In any case, six of my interviewees (almost a quarter of the total) hinted at their parents' reservations when it came to identifying with the African American population.

One American-born respondent stated, "My dad told me to say I am Ethiopian when people said I was black." Another Gen 2.0 stated, "My parents do not identify with blacks in America. They say we are Ethiopians and black Americans are as different from us as white Americans are.

But myself? I identify with African Americans despite being Ethiopian." Another respondent who came to the U.S. as a child spoke more negatively. "Ethiopians do not identify with African Americans. Ethiopians view African Americans negatively. We identify only in skin color; beyond that we are very different from them." Overall, however, I found that the 1.5 and 2.0 children of the immigrants hold more positive and open attitudes towards African Americans than their parents do.

When I asked one young man why he thought the first-generation parents held more negative attitudes, he said, "My ethnic group doesn't like to be identified with the African Americans because of the stereotypes."

> My parents do not view themselves as African Americans. They view African Americans as violent, just what they hear and see on the news. They would say Do not dress like them, ear piercing, etc. They say Stay away from them. But I know there are good African Americans; they are not all like that.

Some in the parent generation believe inner city African American culture does not value education and they want to protect their children from such influence. For this reason, parents attempt to create distance and separation. I must note that the concern of parents is not baseless. My respondents described attitudes they observed in the African American community:

'Education is not a high value if you strongly identify with the African American community.'

'Taking on black racial identity can play a role in one's focus on educational success. Many in that community view the educational effort as hopeless. It gave me an excuse to not do so well.'

All my interviewees emphasized the high value that the immigrant community places on education. In fact, in most cases this high value became a source of pressure and conflict between the parents and their immigrant children. One young woman stated:

> I am determined to succeed in school ... I know that mom will kill me if I mess up. We came here for a reason. My mom left everything for us to come here ... All Ethiopians are hardworking and successful. But I was messing up, going with the wrong crowd. I wanted to be more American and never liked to talk to my family in Amharic. I was lost. My mom never liked it. I almost had an emotional breakdown as I was trying to fit in and also trying to succeed in school.
>
> I wasn't thinking of social things or friends ... Friendships were not a priority. The priority was you have to adjust, go to school and get good grades because your parents tell you that's why you came here. I remember thinking: Go straight home and

focus on school ... because you are in this country for a purpose. You are here to go to school and make your life better. It doesn't matter if it bothers you; you are an Ethiopian. I suppressed my personal feelings until I was an adult.

Another interviewee said: "My mom prefers that I make white friends or even be like whites, rather than blacks." What do we make of such statements? From the parents' point-of-view, it's a strategy to encourage their children to enter middle-class American society and protect them from joining an underclass.

THEME 3: American-ness

Twenty-three of the twenty-five participants in my survey labelled themselves, 'Ethiopian-American,' or bicultural. What did they mean by that?

The bicultural label is elastic—it stretches to include the creation of a national American + Ethnic identity for immigrants from any country in the world who wish to identify in this way. At the same time, it offers a cultural identity for those who don't wish to be called American yet but also know they are different from people in the Old Country. For Gen 2.0, born in America, all they know is this country, while Gen 1.5 has lived longer in the U.S. than in their country of origin and American society has shaped their social and cultural experience more than the Old Country has. For recent immigrants, 'to be an American' means holding onto a racial ethnic identity, if one is not white.

Twenty-three of the twenty-five interviewees identified as American in nationality but all twenty-five also claimed American cultural identity!

The interviewees speak positively when they call themselves that. One Gen 1.5 man who immigrated at age eleven stated, "My identity is Ethiopian American. I fit better in the American culture. I feel belonging. To be specific, I fit better with African Americans." Like this interviewee, all twenty-five interviewees emphasized they are mostly more comfortable and competent in American culture than they are today in Old Country culture. Where would they choose to live, in America or Ethiopia? "I am too American to be Ethiopian.... I will say I am Ethiopian American; Ethiopian by heritage and American by culture and nation," one man said. In response to the question, "Where is home for you?" the Gen 2.0 group (born here) and those who immigrated at a very young age (under five years) always answered, without hesitation, "America."

On the other hand, most of the Gen 1.5s, when asked 'Where's home?' responded 'America,' but I heard doubt or hesitancy from some of them. One Gen 1.5 who immigrated at age twelve said:

> I don't know where home is. I kind of view America as my home. I will go back for visits, but I will not go to live there [Ethiopia]; I am Ethiopian

American. If I go back [to Ethiopia] I know I will be out of my element. I think I can live there [Ethiopia] but I won't be comfortable.

Only two participants stated ambivalence in identifying as American. One participant detested America's war in Iraq. The other stressed a difficult assimilation experience with regard to race. She still clings to her childhood friendships. She said she would pack up and go back to Ethiopia, provided a job in her field becomes available.

Nevertheless, all the participants said their future is here in America. As stated earlier, all participants acknowledged they are culturally American. The level of comfort they express in the American culture, versus comfort level expressed in Ethiopian culture and language, supports this. Their social lives are rich with multiracial and multiethnic friendships, evidencing their assimilation. This is all consistent with being a 'bicultural person.'

Despite ambivalence over race-labelling and ethnicity, most of the survey members believe their future in this country is bright and positive. Thirteen of the twenty-five expressed big hopes for success in this society.

"Race really doesn't bother me," one interviewee said. "I do not believe it will stop me from succeeding in America. It is up to me to work hard and succeed." Another young man said, "I don't believe race or ethnicity will hinder me, not nowadays. We are getting close to having a black president." (This interview took place in early 2008. I only wish I could have heard his thoughts on the election of Barack Obama as U.S. president that fall.)

A second young man said:

> I am optimistic about the future. I believe I will succeed in this country. My brother is an example.... Nowadays racism is less and as a result it won't hugely hinder one's future progress. Of course, one may need to work twice as hard.

As the youngest of three brothers, this man has seen one brother succeed in Corporate America after graduating from an Ivy League university. His second brother got in trouble with the law and, unfortunately, is on a downward path. His conclusion: 'Success depends on me. Being black doesn't necessarily hinder a person.'

The parent generation has done their job well. Interviewees overwhelmingly base their optimism for the future on two values stressed by their parents: Hard work and the value of education.

A typical response I heard ran like this: "Despite racism and prejudice, I feel very positive about my future in this country. There is opportunity for those who work hard. I expect obstacles because of race and ethnicity but I will be able to overcome through hard work "

The majority believe education is key to success in American society. "Education has played a big role in my assimilation process," one man told me.

Education plays a big role in America…. [The] neighborhood I grew up in was not good and not the school as well. My parents made sure I went to a better school out of our area. That helped me see a different world. My exposure to this side of America impacted me tremendously, causing me to Americanize more than those Ethiopians who were only exposed to Inner City African American culture. There are really two Americas; two worlds. People do not want to say it but there are two worlds. It is not so much black and white as it is one class separated from the other. It is all about money. It is a mindset. Even though I am not financially well off today, my mind thinks on that level where I am driven to succeed. I see improving life for myself through education and business.

A young woman credits her drive to succeed in this country to her parents' sacrifice and expectations:

Education is the ticket to assimilate. Our parents came here to give us a better life, and I feel like education is the key. It has always been emphasized in my home. This is what motivates me and pushes me; because they work so hard to give us an education which is going to push us to further our culture, ethnicity and help our people. I feel it is a steppingstone to move up…. I have grown up in two places: Suburban America and Ghetto America. I have experienced the sense of hopelessness, which is common in the Ghetto, with bad schools where you learn nothing, and I have also experienced the comfort of suburban America with great schools and opportunity. God literally pulled me out of that downward condition when I moved to Denver to live with my sisters.

Her contrast of life in suburbia with ghetto life dramatizes the potential of downward mobility for the children of immigrants. Some respondents gave unsettling answers to my questions. This potential for *segmented assimilation* threatens the future of this population.

Every one of my interview participants has earned a high school diploma. College, however, is a different story. Only eight have graduated from a four-year college, with two of these in graduate level programs. Three interviewees were enrolled, at the time of our interviews, in full-time four-year college programs. The remaining fourteen held only a high school diploma. While fourteen of the survey group are employed full-time, only seven hold professional positions that earn a middle-class income.

None of the interviewees opposed or debated the contribution of education to success in America. However, several believed the college route might not be good for everybody. One young man who completed his GED on his own stated, "Education is important, but I do not know if it is for everybody.... I will start college soon." Another young man in his late twenties, without a college degree, reflected the same attitude. "Education is valuable," he said, "but I am not sure college is for everyone. I myself didn't appreciate education until later on; that is, after I came to the Lord." Still another young man who only has high school pointed out the presence of an attitude among 1.5 and 2.0 Ethiopians when it comes to education and success. He stated, "My parents kept the pressure on us about school. They knew education opens doors of opportunity. But some kids are minimalists. They will assimilate only to the level where they feel some success and then they stop." A U.S. born young man stated how little he thought of education, because he believed there were other ways to succeed in America besides education.

One woman stated her conviction that Ethiopians value education a lot more than the typical American does.

> In contrast with Ethiopians, Americans do not value education as highly. People without degrees get great jobs here, only on experience. When I was younger, I didn't value education as much. I was heavily influenced by the American culture. Now I see how important it is. I am planning to move to Concord, California from Hayward, California, to give my son a chance for good education. Hayward schools have one star, while Oakland is zero. On the other hand, schools in Concord have nine or ten stars.

Based on my survey, showing fewer than half with college completion and only a third in a professional field, *segmented assimilation*—with a sizable population moving on a downward social path, clearly threatens the generation of immigrant children, both the 1.5s and the 2.0s.

I will close this section with a chart that shows the complexity of the identity experience for my twenty-five interviewees. The chart shows how many individuals own each of the three possible identities.

Bicultural Identity (Complexity of Identity)

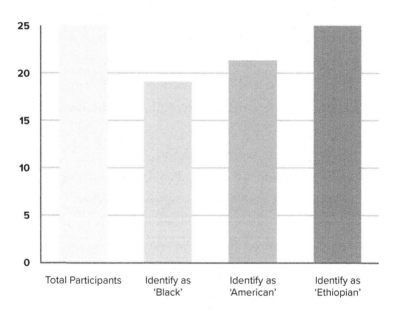

Ethiopian immigrant young people need to negotiate these three major identities. I heard a lot of ambivalence in the interviews. I heard a lack of full acceptance of the three identities or the expression of being an "outsider" regarding one or all three identities.

Interviewees expressed lack of acceptance from Gen 1.0, their parents, because of cultural differences. Some emphasized that African Americans do not see them as fully black. Most of them feel the challenge of being treated as minority by American society despite their identity claim as American. This leads to a discussion of our next major theme.

THEME FIVE: In-between and In-Both, the Hybrid Identity

Let me summarize my findings to this point. My interviewees value their ethnic heritage and identify with their ethnicity. However, many of them reported lukewarm acceptance from the Ethiopian ethnic community and discomfort relating to the American host society. The second research question investigated the American experience—experience in American schools, the impact of race and skin color and identification with the U.S. and American culture. Although most of the interviewees described negative experiences resulting from encounters with racism, all of them affirmed that they identify as Americans.

In the third question we look at **How do 1.5 and 2.0 Ethiopians in America describe the impact of their ethnic community and the American host society on their identity?** I break this down into two sub-questions:

- *How do 1.5 and 2.0 Ethiopian immigrants describe their identity?*
- *How do 1.5 and 2.0 immigrants describe their social and relational world?*

One young woman told me:

> It is kind of confusing because you cannot balance two things out. When you try to go for one culture you still have the presence of the other ... I want both Ethiopian things and American things. I like both American and Ethiopian culture. Part of me is American and part of me is Ethiopian. I love being both; but if I have to choose, I am Ethiopian. At home and at church I am Ethiopian, at school and workplace I am American. I am in between.

This 1.5 young woman uses words like *confusing*. She talks about *balancing* two identities. Despite the confusion, she says she likes both "American and Ethiopian things" and "loves being both." She also sees herself 'playing a different part,' depending on where she is and what she is doing. In church and home, she says 'I am Ethiopian.' At work and school, 'I am American.' As a 1.5 who immigrated at age eleven, she says she will stress her ethnic side over her American side if she is forced to choose. Yet she concludes by saying "I am in between."

This feeling of being a double person, or, as one interviewee put it "I am divided," is a feeling that all the respondents described when they spoke about their identity and how it impacted their cultural and social lives. One 1.5'er stated, "Inside me, I think I am Ethiopian but when I look at my outside, I have lost the culture and the language.

I really am African American." She sees herself as a split person, it seems.

One young man states:

> I know both the Ethiopian culture and the American culture. I have one foot in the Ethiopian culture and the other foot in the American culture ... I find myself right in between because I understand both. I am Ethiopian American. I am both Ethiopian and American and I can't separate the two because it is the fabric of what I have become.

A Gen 1.5 generation young woman said:

> My identity is half Ethiopian and half American. My interest in my ethnic group came later in my life. At first, I didn't like being Ethiopian and tried very hard to be American. I guess after succeeding in becoming American culturally, I lost my accent. When I matured, I felt that I can be both, take the best of two worlds. I do not have to be American because I am not, and I do not have to be Ethiopian because I am not. I realized that my Ethiopian-ness is something that doesn't go away.

In both cultures, she is both an insider and an outsider. She might feel more comfortable if she called herself a global nomad or a sojourner.

How do 1.5 and second-generation describe their social and relational world?

Unlike their parents' generation, 1.5 and 2.0 people swim linguistically and culturally in American life. Exactly what percentage of the individual's social world is ethnic and what percentage is American? The answer will tell us which social space that individual feels most comfortable in, where they hold influence and where they see future opportunity.

With regard to their close friendships, I find the data mixed. Eleven participants said their closest friends are Ethiopians. These participants are all Gen 1.5 immigrants, kids born in Ethiopia but moved here before the age of twelve. On the other hand, fourteen participants stated most of their closest friends are *not* Ethiopian. Seven of them are U.S. born (therefore Gen 2.0's); three were under three years old at the time of immigration; and four immigrated between the ages of four and twelve.

I observed two characteristics about the eleven who said their closest friends are Ethiopians. These eleven are Gen 1.5's, with adequate Amharic skill and comfort in the Ethiopian culture. Secondly, most of them—nine of the eleven—participate in the Ethiopian religious community. Of these, seven identify Protestant and two identify Orthodox.

Interviewees whose network lies within the Ethiopian church appear to have fewer relationships with white and black Americans or non-Ethiopian immigrants. Many of them had more varied social relationships in childhood but went through a change in high school or college. This is especially true for those who grew up in cities where the Ethiopian population is small. One woman stated her experience:

> Ninety-eight percent of my friends are Ethiopians. I do not have a problem connecting with whites or African Americans; I simply choose to be with Ethiopians that have my background. The bond we created with my Ethiopian friends was great. We all went through the same things, came to this country at the same age.... My friends whom I hang out with at the movies, Borders, or coffee shop are all Ethiopians.

She grew up in a city with a large Ethiopian community and had friendship opportunities with Ethiopians from grade school all the way to adulthood. She also connected with people of other ethnicities and native-born Americans. She calls these relationships 'acquaintances.' For her and others like her, maintaining close relationships with the Ethiopian immigrant community is a choice and not the result of inadequate English or inadequate street smarts. In-group ethnics often befriend Gen 1.5's like themselves.

> "Most of my friends now are Ethiopians, about 95 percent.... There are a lot of Ethiopians where I live now [in] Virginia. My friends are Ethiopians like me. They are either born here or came here very young, like myself, speak English and Amharic the same way I do."

Why prioritize relationships with fellow Ethiopian immigrants? One young man gave his reasons:

Since I moved to Denver, my friends are all Ethiopians from the church. It is different to have Ethiopians as friends, compared to the Hispanics I grew up with. I have a lot in common with Ethiopians who grew up here. We all know the language and if we make jokes about our Ethiopians parents, we all laugh about it. Maybe it is easier to sit around and have a good time with Ethiopians. There is an understanding.

This young man grew up in Los Angeles in a very diverse neighborhood and school. However, in his high school years he moved to a new city with a larger Ethiopian population and close relationships with Ethiopians became a possibility for him. As noted above, he found these relationships more meaningful because of the commonalities with in-group kids. Of course, his parents encouraged these relationships, which made the case stronger. However, such in-group behavior may limit meaningful connection with host culture people. Several of my interviewees pointed this out, especially those whose social network is mostly American and non-Ethiopian. These respondents said those whose friends are mostly Ethiopian are not as socially assimilated as they themselves are.

One woman described the trade-off well. "I value getting to know other cultures and connecting with other people outside my ethnicity.... I like to believe my friends are diverse. They are Hispanics, blacks and whites. I make friends like that in school but when it comes to sharing my personal life, it is going to be with those whom I connect the most [Ethiopians]."

She reserved intimate or close relationships to in-group people, yet she also maintained connection with out-group people as 'acquaintances.' All eleven respondents said they valued relationships with people of other ethnicities.

In contrast, fourteen of the twenty-five participants stated their closest friends were out-group people (non-Ethiopians). Seven members of this group are U.S. born; three were under three years old when they came to this country; and four were between ages four and twelve when they came. Respondents in this group say their friends are diverse: whites, African Americans, and non-Ethiopian Gen 1.5 and 2.0 immigrants.

One young man expressed concern about a trend he has seen in recent years. As the ethnic population grows, he said, newly arrived immigrant kids seem to prefer socializing only with fellow Ethiopians.

> My friends are very diverse: whites, African Americans, Ethiopians, Koreans etc. I do not limit my friendship to only Ethiopians or a majority as Ethiopians. The more our Ethiopian population grows, the more some Ethiopians limit their friendship to Ethiopians and that limits their assimilation. It is very important to get to know people from other ethnic groups, because America is a land of diversity.

Close Friends In-Group vs. Out-Group

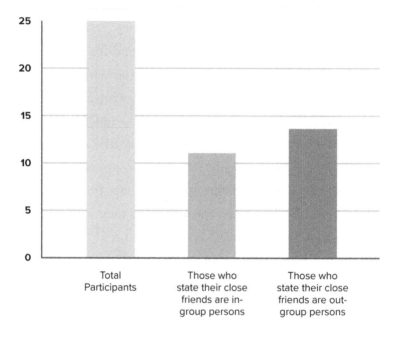

Researcher John Berry devised two questions to identify the 'acculturation strategy' of an immigrant.[91] Question One— Do you value maintaining your cultural heritage? Question Two—Do you value having contact with and participating in the larger society? He asked his survey participants to answer Yes or No to each of these questions. Their answers, Berry said, show us the individual's 'acculturation strategy.' A Yes answer to both questions show a strategy of 'integration;' a No response to both questions shows a 'marginalization strategy.' Yes to the first and No to the second shows a 'separationist strategy,' and No to the first and Yes to the second describes an 'assimilationist strategy'.

Using this test all twenty-five of my interviewees responded with Yes to both questions. See the chart below.

Declared Acculturation Strategy of Interviewees

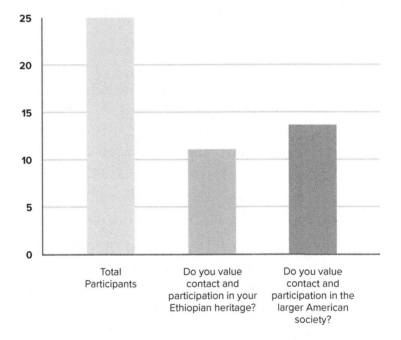

Total Participants

Do you value contact and participation in your Ethiopian heritage?

Do you value contact and participation in the larger American society?

However, looking beyond their answers to the interviewees' actual behavior, the data suggests the majority really practice more of an 'assimilationist strategy' than they are willing to admit. The majority say their interactions and relationships with the American community are closer than those with the Ethiopian immigrant community. All twenty-five participants are more proficient in the host society culture than the ethnic culture. To me, this does not appear accidental. It is the result of a deliberate strategy of assimilation.

Looking at the comfort level in American culture over Ethiopian culture, openness to intermarriage and the personal history of the individuals, the majority of my twenty-five interviewees appear to be assimilating. In fact, it looks like they are in a hurry to assimilate.

THEME SIX: Spirituality
(I use this term to assess the experience of the interviewees in relation to the five questions below)

The theme of "spirituality" organizes the research findings in answer to Question Four: **How do Gen 1.5 and 2.0 Ethiopian immigrants describe their Christian religious experience?** One of the important findings of my research is this: twenty-four of the twenty-five participants state that spirituality or religious practice/experience is important to them.

You will recall that my big driving question, which led me to Concordia Seminary in 2003, was my quest to understand the social and cultural awareness of Gen 1.5 and 2.0 Ethiopian children. I hoped to find clues that might lead me to develop a socially and culturally relevant ministry that could reach them with the Gospel. In what follows, I will summarize the data my twenty-five interviewees provided on their religious identity and experience. Four sub-questions guide my exploration of this topic.

1. *How do they describe their religious experience?*
2. *How do they describe their experience in ethnic churches?*

3. *How do they describe their experience in American, non-ethnic churches?*

4. *What would a ministry that feels socially and culturally relevant look like?*

Religious Tradition of Interviewees

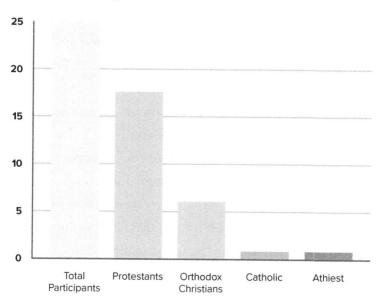

Of the twenty-five, seventeen affiliate or identify as Protestant, six identify as Orthodox, one is Catholic, and the final one is a self-declared atheist. Furthermore, the Protestants divide into the type of church they affiliate with. Eight attend an ethnic (Ethiopian) Protestant church, while nine say they attend American churches. Those who claim Orthodox faith all belong to the ethnic Orthodox Church.

I'll begin with the group that attends an Ethiopian Protestant church. Seven of the eight who affiliate this way say they take their faith and religious identity very seriously. Describing her religious faith and experience one young woman said, "I am 100 percent committed to my religion. I practice daily and weekly activities. I witness my faith and serve in the church. I spend six hours a week in church related activities. Religion is important to me because it is a source of my happiness in all of life." Another described the place of religion in her life as, "Religion is who I am. It is my identity. I would probably be lost without it." Still another said, "Religion gives me a strong foundation . . . My identity is in Christ ... To me race is just about the color of one's skin. It is not about identity. Identity is not about the way your parents raised you and what culture you have; your identity is now in Christ." Another young man described what his faith means by saying, "My religion is very important to me. God loves me and He died for me; that is important."

A young man from an Orthodox family, who 'converted' to Protestant Christianity, said:

> I found my identity in Christ during my last high school year ... I became a Christian based on my personal decision when convicted by the Spirit. Christianity is very important to me. If I didn't find my identity in Christ, I would still be searching. That is the problem with the youth. There is a great void, a hole, in terms of identity. That is why young people are trying to fit in. It is after I found myself that I found the way forward. This is a foundation I

can grow from. Once I found my identity in Christ it was much easier to say This is me; I am a child of God. He formed me in His image. I do not have to be anything else, as long as I am right before Him. My value system is a Christian value system.

A second man with a similar life journey said:

I am a Protestant Christian. Most of my family is Orthodox. There has been a big change in me from four years ago. I am almost unrecognizable today. Filth used to come out of my mouth. I am changed now. I am dignified. I set goals for the future—my life is based on them now. My religion gives me a rich sense of life. It is the centerpiece of my life. My religious identity is more important to me than any other identities I may claim. My religion gives me a way of being with people and a moral grounding. Everything I do and what I believe is based on my religion. For me it is my life. It is the way I conduct myself.

Nine of the seventeen Protestants say they attend a host culture church (American). The religious commitment of this group varies sharply from that of the eight who attend an Ethiopian Protestant church. Of the nine who say belong to American Protestant church, two are highly committed, four are semi-committed, and three are not committed.

Both committed individuals are adult converts whose parents are leaders in an Ethiopian Protestant church. They say the ethnic Protestant church their parents belong to didn't appeal to them culturally and socially, despite the fact that they grew up in that church as children. Although their parents still serve as leaders in the Ethiopian Protestant church, these young men belong to American churches and one of them serves as an elder. When I asked him about his Christian identity, he responded by quoting the words of St. Paul in Philippians 3, where Paul says ethnicity, race, language and any other identity are far less important to him than his life in Christ.

Of the four 'semi-committed' interviewees who attend American Protestant churches, three come from a Protestant background—their parents belong to ethnic Protestant churches. The parents decided to take their children to American churches because their Ethiopian churches did not have an adequate children's and youth ministry. These young men claim Christian identity and speak of attending church weekly; however, their involvement is limited to just that. One described his religious practice and experience as, "I believe religion is very important. It puts things into perspective and gives you confidence. God is watching my back. It is also important not to be an extremist."

Interestingly, all the individuals who today affiliate with American churches come out of a Protestant background. To my knowledge, no Orthodox believer has made the move from his/her tradition to join an American church.

Ethiopian Orthodox believers who left that faith tended to join Ethiopian evangelical churches, rather than American churches. Some Ethiopian Orthodox believers have joined other Orthodox denominations, such as Greek Orthodox, especially when there was no established Ethiopian Orthodox church available in their community.

Six of our twenty-five interviewees belong to the Ethiopian Orthodox church tradition. Four of them are female, two are male. They describe their personal spirituality and affiliation to the church with differing levels of commitment. Using as a yardstick of commitment the following—1. frequency of church attendance; 2. involvement in church activity; 3. personal daily devotion and prayer—three of these six Orthodox Church followers appear to be semi-committed in their church and religious practice and identity.

One of the three young women, whose mother converted to the Protestant faith, expressed her disapproval of her mother's change of church affiliation. She herself has a renewed interest in church, motivated by a recent family tragedy and the help that her family received from the local Orthodox Church. She says, "I was born into the Ethiopian Orthodox church.... You really must not choose a church; you must go to the church you were born into and where your family goes. It was after my brother's death that I began to go to the Ethiopian Orthodox church regularly."

Another young woman, active in an Orthodox church, describes her church involvement completely apart from her spiritual life.

I am an Orthodox Christian. I was born into this faith.... I believe religion is very important.... I never questioned its importance; but it is a very personal thing. When I am involved in church activity, I keep it separate. I have a sense of guarding my faith and do not discuss it, sort of thinking it is mine.... My Christian identity doesn't define who I am. When I participate actively in the church, I do it for the community and the people who happen to be in the church. I do not see what I do as my Christian duty. My motivation is to do stuff for the community and my faith is separate from that. My spiritual progress is personal, and I do not feel the church plays a role in it. I am not a strong Christian.

This individual is searching, I concluded. In the interview she talked about reaching out to Protestant Bible studies occasionally when she faced some spiritual issues in her life. She was searching and refused to be defined by her church.

The highly committed Ethiopian Protestant members and the highly committed American Protestant members appeared very similar in their inside-the-church activities and attendance level. However, on the topic of communicating one's faith, a sharp difference emerged. When I asked members of the Ethiopian Protestant church about sharing their faith with unbelievers, they responded by emphasizing their activities within the church and de-emphasized reaching out to people who are not Christians. "I am a youth leader in my church," one said. "I witness my faith and serve in the church with the youth group," another one said. A third interviewee responded to the question of communicating the faith by saying, "Those of us that are here meet on Saturday and help the youth and the children on Sunday."

On the other hand, members of American Protestant churches with the same degree of religious commitment said, "At my work I will make every effort to let my light shine. I welcome conversations about religion in the break rooms. Spreading the Gospel makes my day." A second person said, "I ... make an effort to reach out to non-believers with the intent to convert them."

It appears American Protestant church members focus more on reaching out to others. Several pointed out that they have a much larger opportunity, simply because language or culture do not limit them, and they feel able to invite anyone and everyone to their American church. One man said:

> I question the 1.5 and second-generation Ethiopians who are in the ethnic church ... With that approach [Ethiopian language ministry] you will have to count mission out. You have very limited audience and opportunity. I am a member of a host culture church. The advantage it gives me is that it provides me a larger mission opportunity. I can bring to church any one I meet and lead them to the Lord. If I was in an Ethiopian church, I would not be looking for that opportunity.

The contrast between Protestant and the Orthodox followers in sharing their faith is significant. Orthodox group members make it clear that converting others is not a goal that they pursue. In fact, they believe that it may be inappropriate. One said, "I don't think I should convert other people. All religions are similar anyway." Another stated, "It [religion] is a very personal thing." Still another young woman told a story of how she was offended by the efforts of a Muslim individual to convert her when she visited the mosque where her Muslim friend attends. She said, "People in my church do not try to convert others; but when I went to my Muslim friend's church, the preacher tried hard to convert us. That was not right, and my friend apologized to me."

1. How do the research participants describe their social relationships in light of their religious identity?

Nine of the seventeen Protestants, who categorized themselves as very committed, said their closest friends are religious like themselves and, most importantly, belong to their religious group. One said, "My friends are all Christians; they have to be." Another said, "My church life and social life are one and the same." These two belong to the Ethiopian Protestant church. Those who belong to an American Protestant church and are also highly committed stated a similar response. One stated, "My closest church friends are white Americans."

Among those who described themselves as semi-committed or not committed, the interviewees said although they may have friends that are religious, their closest friends are either not necessarily Christian or do not belong to their religious group. One stated, 'Most of my friends are African American ... they are not church goers.' Another talked about friends who belong to another Christian tradition and some from another religion altogether. He stated "My Christian friends are Catholics. My mom doesn't like that. But I do not see a difference, we have similar beliefs. One of my closest friends is an atheist. I keep up my friendships with my Buddhist friends as well."

2. How do research group participants describe their experience in the Ethiopian church in America?

Interviewees viewed the spiritual ministry of the first-generation church as a mixed bag. Twelve expressed negative opinions of the ethnic church's ministry to the 1.5 and 2.0 immigrant Ethiopians; ten had mixed feelings about the church's ministry. Only two expressed positive feelings, and these two are not committed to the church.

Of the seventeen Protestants, nine hold negative views about the ethnic Protestant church's ministry to Gen 1.5 and 2.0. Although these nine attended Ethiopian church as children, every one of them said the culture and language of their parents were not for them.

A young man who is highly committed in an American church stated, "I left the Ethiopian church because of cultural barriers. There was no benefit there for me, since I hardly speak the language. Many people of my generation feel the same way. Those who were born in Ethiopia and have Amharic language skills stayed. Most people who attend the Ethiopian church in America attend for cultural reasons." A second young man, whose parents brought him to the U.S. at age eight, said, "What drove me away from the Habesha [Ethiopian] church is the language and culture thing. I do not understand what is going on." This sense of not understanding what is going on is not just a problem for the children born in the States, but many 1.5's, who came here as children, feel alienated because they are not proficient in language and culture.

The result is that many leave. One other young man who has better language and cultural abilities explained his reasons for leaving. "I left the ethnic church where I used to go because my friends left. They went to American churches for better children's ministry programs. Language and culture were also issues for me. It was difficult." These issues cause some to question the priorities of the ethnic church. One interviewee said, "When I think of the Ethiopian church, I think the culture takes over. Do we come together to talk about culture or God?"

Others complained about the length of sermons (average one hour, with the entire service usually lasting two and a half hours) and a sense of not being accepted. "I hated it in the Ethiopian church. The sermons were long and didn't make sense to me. In the Ethiopian church I didn't feel accepted.... I don't fit into the Ethiopian religious community." Another said, "I don't feel comfortable in an all-Ethiopian setting. This is true at church as well. I don't feel a sense of belonging. I don't fit into the Ethiopian church." In addition to the language and culture challenge, these participants stressed that the ethnic church didn't reflect their lives in an otherwise multicultural world.

One highly committed participant in an American church stated his opinion that those who stick with the ethnic church will experience conflict and end up leaving.

> I question the 1.5 and second-generation Ethiopians who are in the ethnic church. It is only a matter of time before they leave. Most will move on and move out. Those staying are those who know the language well. Most who grew up with me in the Ethiopian church have left like I did. If the 1.5 and 2.0 people continue to be part of the first-generation church, they will experience tensions and conflicts.

Despite the appearance of commitment to the ethnic church, these young men and women were not happy and their future in the ethnic church troubled them. One young woman who is very strong in her commitment to the Ethiopian Protestant church stated she wasn't sure she would choose to attend an ethnic church, if she moved to another city. She said, "You shouldn't go church hopping. Church is like a family. You can't switch your family and besides, every church has its problems. But if I have to move to another city I don't know if I will pick another Ethiopian church." One young man offered his solution, "We need a church for us.... At my church, I would like to think there are no boundaries and everyone is welcome, but the truth is, it is for Ethiopians only. Even in the youth group where we do stuff in English, we rarely see people of a different ethnicity or race."

A church for them! A church that is not limited to their own ethnicity! These young people articulate the solution they hope for.

Interestingly, the Orthodox Church interviewees shared similar views. Two of the six hold negative views of the Orthodox Church in America's ministry; two others are conflicted about the church's ministry; and the last two held positive views of their church's effort to serve the 1.5 and 2.0 population, although they themselves are not committed to the Orthodox Church today.

One young woman with a good grasp of the Ethiopian language expresses her frustration over joining the church's choir. She stated,

> I am not a member, but I wanted to be in the choir. I couldn't fit in because of language difficulty. I understand it but it is hard for me when they speak fast. The church is trying. They have translations in English, and I like that. But I am not satisfied.... A lot of us go because it is the right thing to do.... In my church you really can't change much because the older generation would not like the change. They think doing things in English is trying to be American. They say, why be American?

Experience in the Ethnic Church

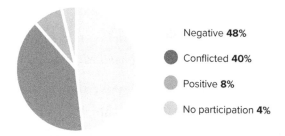

Negative **48%**

Conflicted **40%**

Positive **8%**

No participation **4%**

To summarize, the responses of twenty-two of the twenty-four Christian participants in my interviews ranged from unsatisfied, uncomfortable, and uncertain to outright rejection of the ethnic church, primarily over cultural and social reasons. The data in my research makes clear both Orthodox and Protestant Christians equally share these responses. They state in the clearest terms that, especially after high school, the church's ministry is not relevant. Protestants who worship in the ethnic church were most emphatic about this. Sixteen of the seventeen Protestants said the ethnic church fails to serve the Gen 1.5 and 2.0 population. Up through high school graduation, Ethiopian Protestant church ministry to young people seems to get a passing grade. However, once these young people reach adulthood, they conclude that the church can no longer minister to them.

The Orthodox participants did not speak of youth ministry, outside of the church's effort to teach Ethiopian language and culture. As shown by the pie graph, although the degree of disaffection differs, eighty-eight percent of the participants experience see the ministry of the ethnic church to its children negatively.

3. *How do research group participants describe their experience in American, non-ethnic churches?*

Eighteen of the participants spoke about their experience in American churches. Thirteen are Protestants, four are Orthodox, and one is Catholic. Sixteen of the eighteen stated their experience positively and said they have benefited from the ministry of the American church. (One participant talked about his negative experience in an American church that went through a church split. A second participant said American culture does not fit him. Both individuals, however, are Protestants who are not active in the Ethiopian Protestant church either.)

Many of the respondents held membership in an Ethiopian Protestant church but talked about the contribution of American churches to their spiritual development. They pointedly stated they do not rely on or even expect the ethnic church to meet their spiritual needs. They said this is especially true when it comes to the teaching of God's Word and resources for the church's ministry to children and the youth group. One who serves the youth group in the ethnic church stated, "American churches have contributed to my spiritual development and religious knowledge. Christian media, TV, radio, recorded materials and books have also helped. I have never depended on my ethnic church entirely for my spiritual growth." Another interviewee who served in an ethnic Protestant church said that she attends an American church weekly, in addition to her membership in the ethnic church. She stated, "Because our college group [at the ethnic church] is not strong, for my own spiritual nurture I go to an international American church on Wednesdays."

The daughter of an ethnic Protestant pastor talked about the comfort level she feels in American church gatherings, although she holds membership in the ethnic church. "My Christian identity made me feel comfortable in youth gatherings where 90% of the youth were whites and other ethnicities. This is a contrast with how I felt in high school." In high school she was viewed as black and ethnic but in Christian gatherings she says she was seen first of all as Christian by everyone, regardless of race and color.

Experience in the Host Culture Church

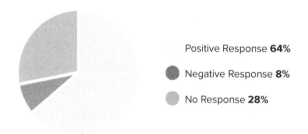

Positive Response **64%**

Negative Response **8%**

No Response **28%**

4. What would a ministry that feels socially and culturally relevant look like, according to the research group participants?

This was not an easy question for the participants to answer. Most of them, Protestant and Orthodox, had not seriously thought about it before I asked the question during our time together.

Description of a socially and culturally relevant church

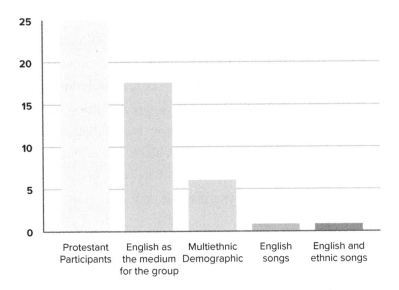

But they made a brave stab at answering the question. Fifteen of the seventeen Protestants said such a ministry must use the English language as its medium. They gave responses like, "My choice is a multicultural church that uses English as its language medium." Another young man said:

> With regard to church preference, I will be attracted to a multiethnic, United Nations kind of church. I can see myself and my friends more attracted to such a church over an all Ethiopian or

American church. [I prefer] a church that embraces the American culture, innovative, a church that doesn't settle on one culture and tradition.

Twelve of the fifteen stated the population or demographic of their ideal church would be multiethnic or multicultural.

A second-generation respondent said, "[The] 1.5 and 2.0 church must be one that reflects our assimilation." A Gen 1.5 interviewee, who currently attends an ethnic church, described what this may look like. "I enjoy Amharic worship and preaching in the English language with 1an American approach. The church for the Gen 1.5 and 2.0 population must have 1) Worship that mixes Amharic and English 2) Preaching in English 3) All communication within the church must be in English 4) A mixture of ethnicities, not just Ethiopians. We are so hungry for that." He seems to be describing a church that starts out with a core of 1.5 and 2.0 Ethiopians and evolves into a multiethnic congregation that reaches out to people of many ethnicities. This, he says, is *"what we are hungry for."*

In summary, my interviewees told me the children of Protestant immigrants are long overdue a church of their own. They are not children anymore and cannot be treated as children by the Parent Generation.

My research calls for the launch of a full-fledged church that ministers to the immigrant children, now adults, with the potential of ministering to the immigrant children of non-Ethiopians and even to the American population of their generation. Unlike the Gen One Ethiopian church of their parents, this church's ministry will connect, language-wise, culture-wise. Like the First Century church in Antioch, this church may introduce a powerful and promising revival to the American Christian landscape.

Real Life Experiments

EIGHT

Tesfai's Unlikely Journey, Part Two

In Chapter Four I told you about Mike Gibson and the Milpitas-based Mount Olive Lutheran Church. My relationship with Mike began before I left for Concordia Seminary to do my doctoral studies. Pastor Gibson and I discussed planting a new multi-ethnic church in San Jose's East Side, reaching out to Hispanic and other ethnicities in that neighborhood. His church would contribute a core group of five or six Caucasian families and our San Jose Ethiopian Church would contribute five or six Ethiopian families. That was our plan and I committed to doing that after my seminary studies finished.

However, during the three years of study, our Ethiopian Church elders got cold feet. They contacted both Bob Newton, our District president, and Pastor Gibson to say they no longer wanted to proceed with the plan. I had resigned my senior pastor position with them, so I had no authority to reverse this surprise news.

Nevertheless, I believed Abby and I should return to San Jose and Pastor Gibson assured me that once I came back, we would continue to work together on a multi-ethnic church plant.

In the Lutheran tradition we have what is known as a call document. Mount Olive prepared a call document to accept me as an Associate Pastor, working as a church planter.

I came onboard in April of 2006 to begin work on the church plant we had discussed. Our model hadn't changed much from three years earlier—Mount Olive would provide a few families as a core group. On my side, although my formal relationship with the Ethiopian Christian Fellowship had ended, I would draw on my connections with Ethiopians in San Jose to recruit some families who might join our effort to plant a new multi-ethnic congregation.

Two months into the plan, I was diagnosed with colon cancer, in July 2006, and in August I underwent surgery. (Fortunately, the doctors detected the cancer early and the surgery eliminated the danger.) As I was preparing for the surgery, Pastor Gibson received a call from a church in Southern California, requesting he consider a call to pastor their congregation. It wasn't anything he had anticipated. Pastor Mike prayed about it, and then he told me he was going to accept that call. In a few short months, the prospects for our church plant had gone from Likely to Unlikely.

As a strong congregational leader, Pastor Gibson had been the person driving the church plant vision within his own congregation. His associate pastor took over, a young pastor fresh out of seminary who is new both to the vision and the church. In fact, he told me: Now that Mike has gone, you will have to lead this church plant as you see it, Tesfai. Those were difficult days. Yes, Mount Olive had called me to do a new church plant, but I was new. They didn't know me very well yet. The congregation agreed to keep me on as an associate as long as the district supported my efforts financially. But as I recovered from my surgery and treatments in early 2007, I realized we would not be able to recruit a core group of families from Mount Olive for the proposed church plant.

Still, I persisted. This church plant would test my own understanding of God's power to create one body of Christ out of different cultures (as I'd seen in the Acts Church, during my studies)!

The district leadership and I went back to the drawing board and as we prayed over this. I suggested we consider planting a multi-ethnic church in downtown San Jose, the heart of this city of one million souls. I knew First Immanuel on Third Street because my good friend Bob Newton had formerly pastored there. Could First Immanuel provide a space that might serve as a meeting place for a multi-ethnic gathering? Yes, the pastor said, we could use their church on Sunday afternoons, when they weren't using it. First Immanuel was right around the corner from San Jose State University. Could we reach out to young Ethiopian students and American students at the university?

To kick things off, I organized a dinner and invited people from a number of congregations, including Mount Olive Lutheran and the Ethiopian churches in San Jose. Close to a hundred persons came to the dinner and I shared my vision of a multi-ethnic church plant, over dinner. After hearing the vision, fifteen or twenty persons, many of them Ethiopians, plus a few Caucasians, expressed interest in the vision.

We launched a Sunday afternoon service at First Immanuel in mid-2007. I hoped the Holy Spirit would shape and equip this group into the nucleus of a church plant team. Meanwhile I looked for a bridge into the University. I found several young Ethiopian and Caucasian students who attended the university and invited them to a Bible study once a week during lunch hour, on campus. I hoped these young people might join the Sunday afternoon Bible Study at First Immanuel and become part of the church plant team. Our sons, Abel and Daniel, also joined the Sunday afternoon meetings.

The Bible study continued for three years. It never grew much larger in number. Ten to fifteen students would gather for meetings, but students are not a reliable base on which to build a church. As they completed their four-year studies and graduated, they moved away.

I thought a lot about ministry to millennials during this period. Did such a ministry fit my skills? Could I identify with them? Could they identify with me? Would I be able to plant a church for second-generation Ethiopians? There were culture differences. We both spoke English, so it wasn't a language problem. But the differences between myself, a middle-aged first-generation Ethiopian immigrant and these very American (although ethnically Ethiopian) millennials in their twenties were real. That's when it hit me: *My role was not to plant a church. My role was to equip young people who would plant the church.*

What should church look like for millennials? Was it better to meet in a church building or would a neutral community space look more attractive to young people? How about a coffee shop, I wondered, if we could afford it, a cafe that would self-support and at the same time, serve as ministry space where young people could hang out and ministry could take place? Or what about a gym? A gym business might pay for itself and serve as a place to conduct ministry.

I floated these ideas with Bob Newton and the District. But as we analyzed the capital required to launch and run such a business, we realized it was much more than we had available. So, that did not go anywhere. I appealed to the local Lutheran (LCMS) churches in San Jose—nine or ten of them—for their assistance in recruiting people to join a church plant team, perhaps loan us some families for a year or two. But these ideas all died, stillborn.

Eventually I concluded my efforts to plant a church weren't succeeding. That felt bad.

I'd succeeded in Sudan. That church took off and ended up planting ten or twelve daughter churches across the country of Sudan. In America, the San Jose Ethiopian Church was already legally organized when we arrived, but it was just a group of young adults fellowshipping. I led the group to form a full-fledged church. It took off and eventually would become the strongest Ethiopian church in the San Francisco Bay Area.

This was the first time my efforts to launch a new church had not succeeded.

But after these four years of experiments, one thing had become as clear to me as the blue skies over California—*my role would not be planting the new church but equipping young people to do the plant.*

As I finished my dissertation, I contacted my old friend, Pastor Hanfere, the Senior Pastor of International Ethiopian Evangelical Church in Washington, DC.

Abby and I had come to know Pastor Hanfere in 1984, when we arrived as refugees from the Sudan. We moved into Silver Spring, Maryland, inside the Capital Beltway that encircles Washington, DC. Ethiopian immigrants were just beginning to come to the US.

People told us about an Ethiopian church meeting at 19th and H Streets in the capital. At the time, Hanfere was not pastor. The group did not need a full time pastor since there were only few people. We joined the group for about five months, until we moved away to Tulsa, Oklahoma.

After we arrived in Tulsa we stayed connected with the Ethiopian community, the evangelical community, in particular. Once a year, the diaspora Ethiopians held a retreat in Chicago. There were no Ethiopian churches yet. Refugees were scattered across the U.S. and Canada and these Ethiopian Christians gathered to encourage one another. By 1984, when we arrived, that conference had grown because the immigrant population was growing. So, we got in the habit of going every year. People there knew me because of my ministry in the Sudan and they invited me to preach and teach at the Conference. And Hanfere attended as well.

My relationship with Hanfere grew much stronger after I was called to pastor in San Jose. I joined a group called the Ethiopian Pastors' Fellowship. By now, there were eight or ten Ethiopian churches across the country and San Jose Ethiopian Christian Fellowship was one of them. Hanfere was one of the Pastors of the Washington DC congregation at this point. (His congregation today is the largest Ethiopian congregation in the country—nearing 1000 members.) I was elected president of the pastors' fellowship and our friendship just kept growing!

I needed to thank him for his financial help during my studies. During our phone call, he said, Why don't you come to DC and share with our church what you learned in your studies? In fact, he said, we need your help. Two of his children—his son Johnny and his daughter Lily—had begun a Bible study for second-generation Ethiopians, Sunday mornings at 10 AM at the church. They were looking for some direction. Could I meet with them?

So, I did. I encouraged Johnny and Lily and the young adult group to consider their direction. Might they be more than a Bible study for second-generation Ethiopians? Might they be an embryonic church? At that moment, however, they could not grasp this concept.

About a year later, Johnny and Lily's brother Paul showed up. Paul had been living in DC, but he hadn't identified with his dad's church or attended the Bible study his brother and sister were leading. Then his personal life went through a transformation. His walk with God changed and he began to attend the young adult group. From the start, he showed interest in leading.

Paul was the youngest. When Paul came in 2011, Johnny and Lily offloaded the leadership of the young adult group to him, and he happily took it on. I saw his hunger for the Word of God and his leadership character—his desire to step out. He quickly began to preach and teach. It did not take very long until he was fully engaged in ministry.

From that point, I focused my coaching on Paul. Sometimes we met online and sometimes I would fly to Washington, DC and spend the weekend with Paul and the entire young adult group. We'd check into a retreat place, and I worked on leadership development and picturing with them what they could become.

Shortly after my realization that my role wasn't planting but equipping young people to do the plant, I landed on the story of Mordecai and Esther while I was preparing a Sunday morning sermon. Here was a young woman, who could pass as a Persian and become the Queen of Persia. She was bicultural, like our second-generation Ethiopians! Mordecai took her under his wing when she was orphaned. He took her in, invested in her and believed in her.

The second thing I saw in Mordecai was his ability to be close to the palace court. He didn't close himself off to the larger Persian Community. He had his ears close to the ground, so to speak. He got information. That's how he was able to realize opportunity, when it came.

As a first-generation person myself, I perked up at this. Mordecai was a first-generation immigrant, it appears, but rather than ghettoizing himself in the immigrant Jewish refugee community, he followed the news in Persia. He didn't isolate himself from the larger society—that by itself, I thought, was unusual.

I saw myself in Mordecai—in his stance of openness to the host society, his knowledge of the Persian culture and his willingness to participate in it. My role would be raising young people who had the advantage of the American/Canadian/ British culture and the language. If they took part, they could make a dramatic difference and impact this society. Like Esther, who ended up blessing not only the Jews but the entire Persian population.

Meanwhile, I continued my work with Paul Hanfere and his Young Adults. He had inherited a group focused on young adult Ethiopians, but their English-language gatherings were attracting non-Ethiopian young adults as well. However, these people would come only once or twice and after that they didn't come back. Why was that? We analyzed it. Ten AM Sunday morning at Pastor Hanfere's Ethiopian Church, as Paul and his young adults were gathering, a thousand or more Ethiopians were arriving at the same time for Ethiopian services. Perhaps those non-Ethiopians felt like fish out of water. I suggested moving their gathering to a Sunday afternoon meeting to see how that would work. They listened and decided to try that.

I pushed further: "Look, you are still like children living in your parent's house and you don't want to leave and stand on your own. You are still totally looking up to the Ethiopian church. And the first-generation population is happy. They don't want you to go. They want you to stay in the space they have provided for you.

"But you realize, don't you," I told them, "That you have already become a church and it's silly to think your identity is limited to the second-generation English-speaking young adult Ethiopians. You've told me you want to be a group for all people. For that to happen, you need to move out of the First-Generation Ethiopian church and stand on your own."

Paul and Christina married in 2016. I sat down with the two of them and talked about a plan to move out of Pastor Hanfere's Ethiopian church within a year. I coached them through setting up a schedule, developing resources, looking at possible venues for meetings and recruiting leaders. They also attended the church planting seminar about that time. The church Pastor Hanfere Senior leads is part of the Assemblies of God. Paul and Christina made a connection with the Assemblies and through his dad's connections, they went to the church planting seminar and that became a very good tool for them.

My conversation was always with the Young People and with Pastor Hanfere, Senior. The young adult group which was called "Next Gen" led by Paul and Christina with the support of Pastor Hanfre Overflow church plant was approved although some first generation leaders and parents were unsure of letting the young people to move out. Of course, those who were unsure are very thankful now as they see the success of Overflow City Church. Overflow not only reaches their children, but other second-generation immigrants. I'm talking about non-Ethiopians who are not Christians. New souls are coming to Christ—they see it!

Overflow Church still, by and large, attracts Ethiopians and Eritreans, so I encourage them to tell their church members to reach out to people in their workplaces who are non- Ethiopians and invite them to come.

I also encourage them to open leadership positions for the Caucasians and African Americans who are coming. Involve them, I said. Give them visibility upfront in the leadership so that other people who are not Ethiopian will identify with them and feel welcome. They're doing that. A young woman has joined the leadership team who is not African American, but African. They have a Caucasian drummer in the band.

Three church plant stories follow this chapter—three churches in which, by God's grace, I played a role in their launch. What should readers look for in these three church plant stories? What lessons might be there?

First, there's the negative lesson. The first-generation Ethiopian leadership has failed so far to grasp the vision of a second-generation church. You'll find that true across the board. Even in Pastor Hanfere, Senior's church, it took several years for things to happen, although it was also true that Paul's development may have taken that long anyway.

But note the resistance or lack of understanding of the vision by the first-generation. There is reluctance to let the children run their own church.

When I do public presentations, I sometimes use a PowerPoint image to illustrate this. I tell the story of a farmer who plants a large field of pumpkins. The farmer gets curious early on, as he visits his field. He sees this one little pumpkin coming out, still about the size of a grain of corn, and he decides to rescue that little thing and he puts a glass two-quart jar over it to protect it. A couple of months later, he goes out to see his pumpkin field and, in all directions, it's all orange and beautiful. Then he kinda remembers that little corn-size pumpkin that he put in a jar. And he goes and finds it.

Every one of the pumpkins in his field is large and round. However, the little corn-size pumpkin that he put under the jar to protect it has grown to the size of the two-quart jar and stopped because the jar prevents it from growing any further. I use that story to illustrate how we, the first-generation, can limit the second-generation from reaching what God had in mind for them.

Why would the first-generation do that? Perhaps it is unknowingly, or perhaps out of fear and insecurity, not knowing what the end product might look like, and they cross the boundaries of culture and ethnicity to lay down limits.

The other thing is the young people themselves. In all three chapters that follow this story, in the churches where I have come as a mediator—Washington, London and

Toronto—the young people are very dynamic. They are also very loyal and appreciative to their first-generation parents. Sometimes they are blindly loyal, as in: We don't want to disappoint our parents so we will submit to any limits our parents lay down.

One more lesson I see is the importance of trust level. In the case of Pastor Hanfere and his son, Paul, the trust level is strong. Hanfere Senior's willingness to trust his son's leadership is visionary.

In the case of Ephrem (London Church) and Heskias (Toronto Church), we see two young leaders who lack the relational strength and trust with the leadership of the first-generation churches. Trust needs to be cultivated, or you need a first-generation leader willing to take a chance and believe in his young people. Such first-generation leaders are rare.

There are some good reasons why the first-generation is reluctant or even unable to trust their children, because of the way they perceive millennials. As Heskias says in the Toronto story, the parents see their kids graduating from college and returning to live in the parents' basements. They see their children getting older and not marrying. And they wonder can we trust young people like this to take over our precious church, our Little Ethiopia?

It's also a fact that the first-generation looks critically at American Christianity—as very different from the Christianity of Ethiopia. The American church service lasts an hour. Ethiopians have a two to three-hour service. The American church seems to be a once-a-week deal, for one hour, and after that people scatter. For Ethiopians, church is very involved and very connected with daily life and there is a heavy emphasis on prayer. Worship services are not strictly structured. They are more fluid, with a strong emphasis on letting the Spirit move.

Many Ethiopian first-generation leaders don't realize that some of these practices are cultural. They say very little about how spiritual a person or church really is.

There may be a spiritual element to Eastern Christianity's emphasis on the Holy Spirit and trust and faith (*see Glossary for a definition of 'Eastern Christianity'*), whereas Western Christianity has been very, very practical and pragmatic, rather than emotional or spiritual. But when it comes to how one lives his life, how a person displays Christ-like character, the difference between Eastern and Western Christians is not large. The Christian walk is about commitment to a Jesus way of life.

I don't believe Ethiopian Christians are necessarily more committed to Jesus than American Christians. They just have different habits that grow out of their culture. But most Ethiopian Protestants don't see it that way. They see long hours of worship in church and long hours of prayer or emotional experiences as 'spiritual.' To me, the test of spirituality is obedience. And I see a lot of disobedience in both Ethiopian and American Christians.

NINE

Washington, DC:
The Overflow Success Story

The YouTube video on the church's website shows the face of the Regal Majestic Theater, a three-story that curves and reaches toward you like the prow of a ship. The lower half is all boxed plate glass and shiny aluminum. Above, the block letters spell out **M-O-V-I-E-S,** but no moviegoers are queued up to buy tickets today. It's Sunday and someone has erected a white vertical banner in front of the plate glass, where it flaps in the morning breeze. The banner reads **OVERFLOW CITY CHURCH.**

The video rolls. A male voice whispers intensely but the words come muffled. On the dark screen, we can make out lovely brown hands, lifted and framing a stage filled with guitars, cymbals, vocalists. Certainly not a rock concert. Might it be a Christian worship song? Cut to a wide-open face and a woman laughing: 'We're family!' she cries to the face she reaches for and hugs. White script unrolls across the dark screen, a word at a time:

OVERFLOW CITY CHURCH
IN SILVER SPRING, MARYLAND
A LOT CAN HAPPEN IN ONE YEAR

The camera blurs over a blue tank and that's a man's head, falling backward with the baptizer's hand covering his nose and mouth and now his head emerges, scattering water in all directions while the baptizer lifts wide-open hands. Behind him, a young woman claps enthusiastically, and the script runs on:

120 NEW SALVATIONS
18 BELIEVERS BAPTIZED

"Climbing up a tree out of hunger!" The voice says. We see him clearly now, the baptizer again, a bald thirty-something with a shadow beard, coat-less and his shirttails hanging out over his Levi's. A battery pack sprouts wires out of his back pocket, and he speaks into a Lavalier wrapped around his cheek, leaving his arms free to gesture right and left as he strides about the stage. "Zacchaeus! And Jesus, walking ahead of the crowd, stops. There is something about positioning yourself in hunger that begins to draw, to pull on the presence of God in your life!"

The audience in the ranked, vertically tiered seats stands now. They sway with the rhythm that the female vocalist croons into her mike, onstage.

The YouTube video feels very 'millennial.' It drips with media-savvy, with touchy-feely enthusiasm and flesh-and-blood closeness that doesn't feel like 'church'. The atmosphere in the theater seems a world apart from church bulletins and creeds.

———

Six months after that YouTube video was shot, 'the baptizer'—Paulos Hanfere—and his wife, Christina, talk about the birth of their church, Overflow City Church of Silver Spring, Maryland. Does Paulos consider himself an Ethiopian? Or an American? Or an Ethiopian-American?

"I still haven't quite figured that out," he says. "Maybe you can help me with that. I would say Ethiopian American. I would say my roots are Ethiopian, but I've spent so much time here in America that I just consider myself an American. I was born there, yes, but my parents brought me when I was five months old."

His English is polished and devoid of foreign accent. Which part of him is Ethiopian?

Paul Hanfere finds it ironic that he's the lead pastor of an urban church. He told a reporter from the Assemblies of God newspaper that "pastoring was never on my grid. I thought I was going to work in the marketplace.' So, he hired on as a Project Manager for Dell Computers after he graduated from college.

Church had never been an interest to Paul. "I really wasn't that close with the Lord when I came out of college. My dad pastored an Ethiopian church here in DC, with

Ethiopian language and Ethiopian customs. We had an English worship service. So, I signed up to help with the Young Adult ministry, catering to folks in my situation, whose parents were Ethiopian.

Paul's older brother and sister led the young adult ministry but after he'd been a part of it several years, they both simultaneously pulled back from leadership to focus on building their families. So, Paul stepped forward to take the lead. He quit his job at Dell, sold his car, gave away his possessions and set off for ministry school. He talks about the defining moment that happened next.

"So here I was worshiping by myself one night," Paul says. "I had my Bible open, my eyes closed, not praying, just really focusing on the Lord. I was just beginning to worship God, and I began to see with such clarity, in such vividness, the faces of individuals that I had never seen before. They were flashing before my face. One face, after another, after another, after another. Some were old. Some were young. Some were white, some black, some Hispanic and other ethnic backgrounds ...

"As this is going on, I get an impression in my heart—which I believe to be the Lord—saying, 'Son I want you to gather my lost sons and daughters.' And at that, my heart bore witness that it was God speaking to me. To be honest, I didn't know what exactly that would look like. I wasn't planning or intending to plant or launch a church. I wasn't even planning to become a pastor, for that matter. I simply felt a need for training to do a better job of leading our group.

"But the seed implanted in that encounter with God produced a big crop. Fast forwarding years from there I can say what He meant when he said 'gather my lost sons, and daughters.' It meant planting a church that was multi-ethnic and available for all people."

Urban legend has it that mixed-race children are more beautiful or more talented, like Halle Berry or Barack Obama. Christina Hanfere, Paul's wife, qualifies. She radiates—her luminous eyes in the perfectly oval, perfectly olive-toned face and the tumble of glowing black hair conjure up Elizabeth Taylor as Cleopatra. Christina was born in Athens, Greece to an Ethiopian mother and an Italian dad, who parted ways with the family after she was born. Like many Ethiopians in the period of the Civil War, most of her family had already emigrated to North America so Christina's mother moved there to join the extended family, when her daughter was eleven.

As co-founder and associate pastor of Overflow Church, Christina today leads worship, the discipleship ministry, and takes turns teaching and preaching. What about her identity? Does she consider herself an Ethiopian-American or an Italian-American?

"I'm a very, very proud Canadian!" Christina says. "Even though I was born in Greece, I just relate more to the Canadian culture, to the Canadian way of life. I'm a Canadian Ethiopian, I suppose. I did grow up in an Ethiopian home. My Mom is Ethiopian. But, in terms of just culture, mindset, traditions, values, a lot of that stuff came to me from the Canadian culture.

In fact, she speaks Amharic and even interprets for Paul, whose Amharic skills are minimal. They met through a mutual friend, the worship leader of the young adult ministry Paul was leading, by now, at his father's church.

In fact, the church Christina attended in Toronto had a strong relationship with Paul's father's church in Washington, DC. The church sponsored regular ministry trips to Washington. She got to know people in the group that Paul was pastoring. One of those individuals was the worship leader, who eventually introduced them to each other.

"He was convinced Paul and I were a match for each other. We had a lot in common. The biggest thing was our huge passion for ministry.

"I had my very first encounter with God when I was thirteen years old," Christina says. "My mom was adamant I attend this church conference. I didn't really want to go because it was an adult conference. Just being thirteen, I thought: No, this is not for me. But my mom was adamant: You have to go. You have to get prayed for.

"At the end of that service, the guest speaker said God was impressing on his heart that he should pray for all the children. My mom insisted I go up and get prayed for. So, I did. And in that moment, I had my first encounter with God. I received the very first prophetic word in my life. It was more than a word. It was very detailed and specific. Details—like you're gonna lead a ministry, and there will be people from many different backgrounds. It's going to represent people from different generations and different backgrounds. It's not going to be in this land. I am going to lead you to a different place for this ministry. I remember these bits and pieces and feeling Whaaaaat? This is way too much for me to comprehend. I was just thirteen!

"But in hindsight, wow, it makes so much sense. Into my teens and my early twenties, God used different people to remind me of the call that He had revealed to me as a 13-year-old girl. Seeing now how so many of those things God spoke of have come to pass, I'm amazed!

About this time, Pastor Tesfai entered Paul and Christina's world and he conducted their marriage counseling. Long before he had known Aligaz Hanfere, Paul's father, as a friend and fellow First-Generation Ethiopian pastor. He visited Hanfere, Senior's International Ethiopian Evangelical Church (IEEC) in DC many times. When Tesfai resigned his position in the San Jose Church to pursue doctoral studies in Ft. Wayne, Indiana, Pastor Aligaz offered to help financially.

Hanfere, Senior sent a few hundred dollars every month to support Tesfai's studies because he believed in the importance of it. As Tesfai finished the doctoral dissertation, the two pastors talked continuously about ministry to the second-generation. Hanfere, Senior made an offer to Pastor Tesfai: 'Our kids here are starting to meet and talk about a new English ministry. Why don't you come speak to them?'

"Dad always had a heart for reaching a multi-ethnic community," Paul says. "But how could he accomplish that when all of his preaching and worship and teaching were in Amharic?"

At Hanfere, Senior's invitation, Pastor T came to visit the new English ministry at the IEEC. And he asked questions. 'What is your ministry going to look like five years from now?' he'd say. 'Ten years from now?' At that point, it was just for Ethiopian-Americans and group members and leaders were satisfied with that. 'Hey, this is bigger than just you Ethiopian-Americans,' Pastor Tesfai would say. 'You could have a church that appeals to people from multiple backgrounds. Not only could you have it—you should have it because it's the right direction to grow.'

The three talked church-planting details: Hanfere, Senior, Pastor T and Paul, and when Paul married Christina in 2016, she also joined the conversation. Paul and Christina's vision for a multiethnic church ministry and what its impact could be for an Ethiopian church in the U.S as Pastor T coached them.

"We had a lot of questions," Paul says. What was the best way to begin? What about the mother Ethiopian church? How could they engage them in this conversation? Paul remembers the discussions and his questions. "Pastor T's insights were vital. It wasn't just a matter of language; it was about cultural nuances I was not familiar with. Pastor T can speak the language. I'm not talking about Amharic or English, because I communicate with my father in English perfectly well. Pastor Tesfai speaks the language of our culture and 'church language.' Together we pictured a multiethnic ministry."

Under Pastor T's guidance, Paul and the young adult leadership put on seminars for the entire church and breakout sessions with the pastoral leadership team of IEEC to help everyone grasp the new vision. It was a foreign concept. In the eyes of the IEEC leaders, why would the young adults want to leave? What we have here is good! You should do something for your own community. That would be a noble thing to do!

"Right about then Dad told me he'd heard about a great leadership training opportunity," Paul remembers. "He said Christina and I should go. Neither Dad nor I knew it was a church planting seminar. We quickly found out it was training on how to plant a church. Christina and I looked at each other and said: This is crazy! Because we both had had it in our hearts to plant a church, but we didn't know where to begin, where to start."

God was sovereignly at work. The church planting boot camp taught the nuts and bolts of starting up a church. What were the elements a new church needed to have? What did a worship gathering look like? What was outreach going to look like? What teams were necessary to start a church? How should the launch be structured?

"Before we went, we didn't know what we didn't know! We went there and got hope, a newfound vision, and the conviction God was calling us to do this. We left the training camp with tools—*this is what you do first!*"

Shortly after completing the training, Paul received a phone call from Pastor Scott of the Oaks Church in Dallas, the sponsor of the training camp. "I heard you attended our church planting workshop." he said. "I wanted to introduce myself and say if you need any help, please give me a call."

"I had never heard of Pastor Scott or his church before that call," Paul says. "They're a Deep South mega-church—maybe four thousand people at their Sunday services, mostly Caucasian, and we were looking at an urban startup, mostly Ethiopian. There's little they could speak into our situation. But on an organizational level they offered a plethora of wisdom and knowledge and counsel. They offered us accountability and oversight and they offered us financial support."

The Assemblies of God denomination has a fund designed for a start-up church. They made an attractive offer to aspiring church planters. If the church planter could raise 10K, they would match with 10K. If they could raise 20, they matched 20 and so on up to 50K. However, the cash came with conditions. First, the Assemblies of God required an assessment that covered the would-be leader's background, his or her personality, his capacity for leadership, his ability to recruit, her ability to evangelize and share the gospel, her ability to preach and teach. The assessment would take nine hours of interviews.

"We did all the training and they assigned us a coach and together we established a ministry path and a Start Date. Those were the scariest days of our lives. I'd never started a church before and neither had Christina! We put together a ministry plan that was forty pages long. Essentially, it was a business plan with everything in it. Our financial strategy. How we would market our church. What our organization would look like. Once we passed their criteria and chose a launch date, we had to raise the funds. That was another leap of faith. I had never raised more than fifty dollars in my whole life. How about fifty thousand dollars?

"But by the grace of God, we raised what we needed to raise, and they matched the funds! Pastor Scott continued to talk with me. 'As you plant this church,' he said, 'We'd like to connect more deeply as a parent-affiliated church.' He was offering to be our accountability partner."

On September 9, 2018, Overflow City Church 'launched'. Paul and Christina had built a team of sixty motivated and gifted persons, most of them young adults from International Ethiopian Evangelical, his father's church. Three hundred and seventy-one 'guests' showed up that first Sunday, all but twenty-five of them adults.

Silver Spring, Maryland lies inside the Capital Beltway, with 82,000 residents. It is part of Washington, DC's metro population of six million people. As the nation's capital, DC is ranked the most educated and affluent city in the nation. It also has the highest drug addiction and divorce rates, according to Paul. The number of homeless and poverty-level persons is staggering. 'Something is deeply broken in our nation's capital that money, prestige or education can't fix. We believe the answer is the message of Jesus Christ that will change and transform lives.'

They called their launch 'Overflow City Church.' Paul explains how they got the name. "In a time and day when people don't overflow with anything except negativity, anger, bitterness and resentment, God has made a way through his

Son. Jesus said: 'I've come to give you life and life more abundantly until it overflows.' That's John Ten, Ten," he says.

The team vetted many possible meeting places in the metro area before the Launch Date. Traditional venues like unused churches or meeting halls were prohibitively expensive. Who had space available on Sunday morning that they weren't using? The team asked. Well, movie theaters, for one. No one goes to see a movie at 10:30am on a day off work. Theaters are also designed acoustically for sound and for a production that uses music, worship and speaking. In addition, the team thought, it was neutral territory for Unchurched America. For many unchurched peoples, a building with a steeple and cross on top looked about as attractive as a tour of the local cemetery, with its headstones and wilted flowers in vases. But who felt funny going to a theater? Especially since last weekend they may have gone the same theater to watch *Harry Potter.*

The team leased the Regal Majestic Theater at the corner of Ellsworth and Fenton in downtown Silver Spring.

"Honestly," Christina says, "A theater seemed unconventional to me. I grew up going to church in a traditional church building. But when we did our pre-launch research, looking for space, we narrowed it down to this theater. From that day until today, my mind has just been blown away. Every Sunday morning, we come in, worship starts, and the Presence of God comes, and people encounter Him and experience Him and it's like WOW!"

What about the vision of a multi-ethnic church that Paul and Christina had articulated in their web promo nine months before the Launch? In that promotion, Paul said he and his team had six million reasons for launching the church. "Six million people live in the Greater DC area. That's six million lives, six million people living in families, six million God-given destinies that we want to see impacted by the life-giving message of Jesus Christ."

How was Pastor T's vision unfolding? Was their church multi-ethnic, as Pastor T had pictured it?

"Right now, we're at eighteen to twenty percent non-Ethiopians," Paul says. "We want to see that rise to thirty percent. If not more, by the grace of God." The non-Ethiopians are a representation of African-Americans—black folks. Because DC is a city of international embassies, Overflow attracts Africa Africans from the continent, as well. Some immigrants from the Caribbean attend. And some Caucasians, white folks.

What about the eighty percent? Who are they?

"Ethiopian Americans born and raised here," Christina says, "Or moved to the States in childhood and educated here. They are mostly professionals, working in the Capital and its metropolitan areas." What attracts them to this particular church? "We're a very communal people," Christina says. "The eighty percent are second-generation Ethiopians, and they relate to one another, in their roots. Most have come from an Ethiopian background but spent the greater part of their lives in a Western culture.

"There's a sense of relate-ability that they probably can't find in their parents' church, which is one hundred percent Amharic and a lot of us are hit and miss with the Ethiopian language. And if these folks go to an all-American church, perhaps they feel they don't belong, with their background and experience, right? But here, they belong!"

Paul prohibits the use of in-group words, intentionally. He tells the story of 'my dear brother, a white American' who had spent some time in Ethiopia and would make references to Ethiopian culture to connect with his audience. "I told him: 'You're my dear friend. However, a friendly reminder. You can't use those words from the pulpit because it polarizes the group who are not Ethiopians.'" The white brother agreed and responded appropriately.

Nor do they celebrate wonderful Ethiopian feasts of injera and wat, like they do in his parent's church. What kind of food do people bring to their potlucks? "Pizza. Panera sandwiches," Christina says. "Hot wings," Paul adds.

The church passed its one-year anniversary successfully and Christmas Week, 2019, the team launched a second service. From all appearances, Overflow City Church was off to a roaring start and working on its vision.

As Paul and Christina Hanfere consider their experience of launching a second-generation church, they have some advice to those who might be considering such a move.

"Don't do it alone," Paul says. "We live in the YouTube Age. You just YouTube something and then go do it the next day yourself. I don't think church planting works like that.

Find a team to do it and include some folks on it who are further down life's path than you are. Find a coach who can coach you through the process and speak into your life. "

"And do your due diligence," Christina says. "Don't think that just because you have a good idea that it will automatically work out. Make sure that it's God's idea, not just a good idea. Make sure that God is truly calling you to plant a church, and you're not just doing it because you love God.

London, U.K.:
A Church Planted in Adversity

2020 COUNTDOWN. LET'S START THE DECADE WITH A BANG! The promotional announcement on their website declared.

In the old brick warehouse at 15–27 Brittania Street near Kings Cross Station in London, forty or so young adults are doing just that. Around the room, little knots of two and three bend together, on sofas or chairs, and appear to be praying. It doesn't deter the woman in the Puma tee-shirt and striped sweatpants. She leads the rest in an enthusiastic rendition of the Hillsong melody, 'I Will Live, I Will Not Die,' cranking her fist to encourage the singing.

This is low-tech. The sign at the doorway is a 2X2 chalkboard with a handwritten scrawl stating, 'Christ Community Church New Year's Celebration'. There is no stage or theatrical lighting for the three musicians. They stand on the same level as the celebrants and croon into mikes and otherwise there's the guy beating the cajon—a wooden box that he straddles and drums rhythmically with his fists.

The pace picks up. The celebrants resolve into a line, facing the singers, clapping loudly and moving with the music and now we see everyone is keeping one eye on the big digital clock displayed on the TV screen, which counts down the last seconds of the old year from 000.00.00.02 to 01 and then 00. He comes in with both arms raised and says: 'Lord, we bless you!' Where did he come from? The fifty-something man looks a bit out of place among these scrubbed and energetic young adults. They respond to him and the announcement of the new decade with loud cheers. They run about, hugging each other. At some point, the group starts up the chorus and they reform their line and chant the chorus about God fighting for us.:

The celebrants dance and thrust their palms upward, as if the darkness hovers there, above their heads, and they can push it back as they sing about lighting up the Kingdom.

The guys raise their fists and begin pogoing, bouncing vertically to the beat of 'Shout it out.'

The fifty-something man is Dr. Ephrem Sahlu. He's clearly at home with young adults. He wears his hair buzzed, wears black horn-rim glasses, carries his stuff in a backpack and grins infectiously.

Ephrem and his young adults hived out of the Ethiopian Christian Fellowship Church at 178 Kings' Cross Road in 2017. The ECFC is only a few minutes' walk away. In this massive, very ecclesiastical looking building, the worship and preaching are conducted 100% in Amharic. The separation was painful, a turn-of-events that Ephrem hadn't wanted.

He'd served at ECFC for twenty-plus years. He'd worked as an usher, a deacon, a committee chair, two terms as an elder, project manager and church administrator before the elders asked if he would consider the job that wasn't getting done, ministry to the youth. In 2012 he took over that assignment.

As one of his first actions, Ephrem requested the elders to separate the youth ministry from the children's department and develop it as its own department. He would gladly continue to lead both groups. "We have the embryo of a church here," he told the elders. "The young adults should govern themselves and make their gatherings into a platform to draw other young adults in London to Christ." The elders asked Could he write up his vision of young adult ministry for them to review?

While he mulled their request, Ephrem attended a conference in Las Vegas where he met Tesfai Tesema. Tesema presented his doctoral research results at the conference, including his conviction that second-generation Ethiopians needed their own church. He reviewed the development of the Gentile/Jewish multi-ethnic church in the book of Acts and presented his theological rationale on why the children of Ethiopian immigrants might use the Acts Church as a model for developing their own church. Ephrem concluded ECFC should hear these ideas. He persuaded the elders to invite Tesfai to present at a seminar at the church in London. As it happened, the other speaker was unable to come and so the church spent the entire weekend focused on Dr. Tesema's presentation and ideas.

After Tesema left, Ephrem put it all down on paper, including an org chart that showed how the daughter church he proposed would stay connected to the mother church, remain accountable to them, draw wisdom and direction from them.

'The elders found the whole concept very, very difficult to accept," Ephrem says. 'They desperately wanted someone to lead young adults and they weren't interested in the vision that I believed to be from the Lord. So, they procrastinated on making any decision and the idea died."

In fact, Ephrem marvels today how he ever ended up at a church in big, cosmopolitan London. He had started life in Ethiopia's capital, Addis Ababa, the son of a very traditional Orthodox family. The Derg Communists had overthrown Emperor Haile Selassie and ruled the country at the time he was finishing high school and looking to enter medical school. The Derg cultivated relationships with fellow Marxist governments and institutions throughout the Eastern Bloc, including communist vassal state Yugoslavia. Ephrem won a scholarship to a Yugoslav university. Alone in Yugoslavia, he flailed about for the meaning and purpose of his life. When he exhausted his search without finding an answer, he looked at ways to end his life. 'That's when I met the Lord, in a communist country!' Ephrem marvels today. A Nigerian colleague led him to the Lord and introduced him to a coterie of African Christians who fellowshipped in the country's one Pentecostal church. But the end was coming. In 1989 the Serbs elected Slobodan Milosevic party leader and president of Serbia, one of the states in the federation of Yugoslavia. Milosevic would push Serbian nationalist policies that would contribute to the breakup of the Yugoslav federation and lead to a decade of civil war.

Ephrem smelled the trouble coming. In 1990, after graduation and a year of medical internship, he moved to London. London was Step One. His larger plan was to move to the U.S., and California, where his sister lived. He began practicing medicine part-time in London, while waiting for his registration as a U.K. doctor to finalize. That's when he heard from God.

"I heard it so clearly," Ephrem says. "I wasn't much more than a baby Christian, but I had already developed an ability to hear the Lord speak and I knew this was Him. 'This is not your life path,' He said. 'I want you to engage in the work of My Kingdom.'

"I heard it and I obeyed. I cut all my ties with medicine, took a job in retail, and began to study the Scriptures on my own. The Ethiopian community in central London was just coming together and I joined the newly forming Ethiopian Christian Fellowship Church to reach the Ethiopian-Eritrean community of London and the United Kingdom."

Twenty-five years later, very experienced in all aspects of church ministry and operations now, Ephrem was shocked by the Elder Board's response to the vision for a daughter church of young adults, which he had presented to them. He returned to his work as youth minister and continued to train leaders and a dynamic band of second-generation

Ethiopian-Brits and, as he had opportunity, he continued to share and communicate the vision of a Second-generation Church with them, without making any plans to launch one. By 2017, the group numbered close to seventy-five, with several upcoming leaders.

2017 began tumultuously at ECFC. In April, the entire church leadership was overturned and pushed out by a new board of elders. The new board was certain about one thing— the possible second-generation church that the young adults continued to discuss was not something they would endorse. The new board delivered a letter to Ephrem and copied all members of the young adult group. The Board demanded Ephrem renounce his vision of forming a daughter church someday or turn the ministry leadership back to them. (The letter distributed even promised to support him financially if he took the vision elsewhere—somewhere outside of their church and on his own.)

"But I told the Board and the entire ECFC congregation—I don't own this vision. I'm just the messenger. I requested the elders to allow the young adults themselves to attend our negotiations on future directions. Their unwillingness to allow that made the discussions that much more difficult."

In the end, Ephrem resigned. "My last day of ministry at ECFC was October 31, 2017. Our young adults gathered that last Sunday and I told them the church had not accepted our vision, and they had a right, as the leaders of the ECFC, not to accept it. I asked those of us who were leaving the church to stand up and we spoke a blessing over those who were going to stay behind. Then I asked those staying behind to stand and speak a blessing over those of us who were leaving. I left without animosity toward anyone. In fact, I sensed the hand of God in all of it.

"The forty or fifty of us who left regrouped. We registered as a church with the U.K. Charities Commission and named ourselves Christ Community Church, U.K. Immediately, we were able to do things we had not been able to do before. We spelled out our vision: we wanted to see lives transformed by Christ, confidently witnessing and impacting people of all nationalities with our faith. Yes, we were mostly second-generation Ethiopians, but we would reach out to people of all nations. We would take God's Kingdom to the multiple nationalities resident in London. We held three core values, values we believed are close to Christ's heart: we would be relational, missional and prophetic.

"We had already set up home fellowships in the North, South, West, East and Central London, with the whole group now meeting weekly to focus, like the church in Acts, on 'the apostles' teaching, fellowship, Breaking of Bread and prayers.' That's Acts 2:42, of course. Our objective is to grow three to five missional communities—embryo church plants—across London in the next three to five years. They will be people of multiple nationalities.

"I preach and do the bulk of teaching, but we've got three young adult leaders who are training to be elders. They share in the preaching and teaching. We've affiliated with Salt and Light, U.K. Salt and Light networks neo-charismatic evangelical Christians. Salt and Light is international—the U.K., Europe, U.S.A., India, Africa. We are part of the South of England Sphere. We focus on relationship building and supporting each other through shared values and mission.

"These are equipping years. We're not in any rush to reach our goals."

In February of this year, Ephrem Sahlu took an urgent call from a distressed Ethiopian mother living in Frankfurt, Germany. She was desperately seeking help with the ministry to young adults in the Ethiopian Church in Frankfurt. Did Ephrem have any ideas?

"I had previously shared Dr. Tesfai Tesema's work on ministry to second-generation Ethiopians with her. I completely agreed with his research findings. I knew how Dr. Tesfai had served as a catalyst for the changes we made in the London Church. I did not have to think twice before I recommended him and his ministry to my friend in Frankfurt."

ELEVEN

Toronto: The Long Path

The building where the Ethiopian Evangelical Church (EECT) meets at 2275 Markham, Toronto, looks like a typical Silicon Valley tilt-up building—all concrete, rectangular, and spacious enough to hold five hundred persons. EECT's Facebook page shows rows of happy faces, some of the women in the traditional Habesha kemis floor-length dress, most in Western clothes. The church website tells the story of its beginnings:

In the wake of the Ethiopian military coup of 1974, the Marxist government killed thousands of people and gave their program a Stalinist motto – the "Red Terror." The government persecuted Christians relentlessly – particularly evangelical believers. They closed down churches. Government soldiers threw Christian leaders and youth into prison and tortured them. As a result, hundreds of thousands fled for their lives to neighboring countries – the Sudan, Kenya, and Djibouti – and from there to Europe, the United States, and Canada.

During this massive migration, the first Ethiopians came to Canada as early as 1985. Ethiopians who settled in the Toronto area established churches in different municipalities of the city. Later, elders of three of those churches came together and prayed to God for his guidance in bringing their congregations together. Thus, the three churches: Bethlehem, Full Gospel and the Ethiopian Evangelical churches united in 1999.

Ethiopian Evangelical Church of Toronto describes itself as 'a congregation of warm and loving, born-again Ethiopian and Eritrean Christians.' While the congregation primarily worships in the Amharic language, a full-fledged English service runs side by side, at the same time.

In 2004, the church hired Brother Heskias Mandelfro to help with the growing second-generation population. Sixteen years later, Heskias is still there. The church recently ordained him Pastor of English Ministries. However, a unique church for the-asecond-generation hasn't happened yet.

Heskias describes himself as 100% Ethiopian. "But I'm an Ethiopian from 30 years ago. I grew up with my grandparents in a very conservative home. So, I've kind of been an old soul all my life.

"I had a God awareness at an early age. (The concept of God is embedded in our Ethiopian culture.) I remember arguing with my grandma about our servants. We had house servants who would serve us at dinner time. The servants would stay in their own rooms and eat by themselves. I argued with her about the justice of God. If this servant bears the image of God, why is he not eating with us? At an early age I had this awareness of a collision between culture and Scripture."

In Grade Four he joined the choir and became one of the leaders of the youth choir, a group of thirty kids, in Grade Five. "I experienced the Baptism of the Spirit just before junior high."

His grandparents were part of a church called Hibret Amba, which was a part of Kale Hiwet (The Word of Life Church). After the overthrow of Haile Selassie's monarchy by the Marxists, people began to flock off the streets into their church. All across Ethiopia, spiritual revival was breaking out.

"I really experienced the power of God and deliverance ministry was a huge part of that, Heskias says. "I remember sitting in this Sunday school room, packed out because we had no fire regulations. They stuck thirty or forty kids into an office built to hold ten adults. Someone walked into our class and said: There's a lot of people here that need deliverance. This is the only room available. Can we please have you leave the room? I raised my hand and said, I'm scared of this person you're bringing in because she is screaming. (It was a demonic manifestation). I said: I don't feel comfortable. So, I walked out.

"But as I walked into this narrow hallway, they were pulling another person out of the service for special prayer. Another demonic manifestation. I had heard our evangelists pray 'in the name of Jesus' for demons to flee. There in the hallway, I found myself trapped--if I stepped forward, this demonized guy would hit me—a very scary man. If I stepped backward, the demonized lady was waiting for me. I said to the man: 'In Jesus name, I command you to get on your knees.' And this military guy, six-foot tall, fell on his knees in front of me.

"And I felt: Oh, this thing works! I said to him: In Jesus name, get up. He stood up. I said: In Jesus name, come follow me. The man followed me. The man was delivered from demonic oppression that day and I felt like a hero. That was my first experience of casting out demons. After that, whenever a screaming incident happened, I got called. We had no leadership development. We were just kids, running around."

The Eighties and Nineties brought an explosion of revival to the Ethiopian Church, especially the Protestant Church. The deliverance Heskias participated in was not a one-time incident. People across the country were encountering the Holy Spirit and coming to salvation. "From that day on, I got very serious about prayer," he says. "By junior high, praying a four-hour stretch was nothing for me. I was the first one in our family who came to Christ. I invited my family, and they all came to church too!"

Shortly after this, Heskias' father moved to Canada, where he already had family. He brought his wife and three children, including sixteen-year-old Heskias, to join the extended Mandelfro family.

Toronto has been a mosaic of cultures for years, long before many American and Canadian cities became so as a result of the loosened immigration laws. "I didn't feel like I had moved to White People's country because it felt like I was living in a refugee camp. Our building had Pakistanis and Filipinos. All the kids in my math class would go next to the ESL class. I was faced not only with post-Christian Canadians, but with the Muslims and Hindus who lived in our apartment building.

"Back in Ethiopia we had prayed about reaching the world. And I remember when we came to Canada, someone prophesied over me: 'The Lord's going to send you across the world and you're going to preach the gospel.' I saw myself as a missionary. I would pray overnight at home and the next morning I went on prayer walks through my apartment complex, praying that the spirits would leave from this home. I prayed for the gospel to touch the people in that apartment.

"I really believed if God would revive Toronto, we could start a revival that would spread around the world. The Filipino family next door--maybe they would call their families in Manila and share Christ. I had Pakistani friends. If we shared Christ here, without getting on a boat or an airplane, I believed I could reach thirty or forty people back in their home country. Salvation revival was a big part of who I was, which translated into street evangelism after I joined a Canadian church. We probably knocked on a thousand doors in a span of three years, doing door-to-door evangelism."

As a fourth grader, Heskias says he heard some sort of voice from the sky. "It was not just a dream. I get teary, just talking about it now. I heard: 'You are mine; you will serve me.' "

He knew something transcendent had happened, but what did it mean? The second decisive step of his call came as he finished Canadian high school. The guidance counselor asked him: What are you thinking, in terms of college or university? "I want to be a priest," he answered. "First I need to make money to pay my bills and eventually I will go to Bible college."

Heskias began studying computer systems. But after completing his final project, he packed his bags and enrolled in Bible college to study theology. Meanwhile, he worked in Information Technology. "Tentmaking work," he calls it. "When I graduated from college, the Ethiopian church asked me to come in and help. That's how I formally joined the team at the Ethiopian Evangelical Church of Toronto (EECT) on a part-time basis."

"They hired me on a 'come on board and help us' basis, because at that time there was no youth ministry in English. This was November 2004. In those days the concept of youth ministry was not clear. Anyone younger than forty was considered to be a youth. And youth still meant Amharic-speaking. The concept of English youth groups did not exist."

The church did not hire him specifically to develop a youth ministry. They were looking for someone to look after the teenagers, so the Amharic service upstairs could go on without interruption. In other words, roles were not clearly defined and we "We did not, as a church, know what we were looking for. To the elders, I was just a young dude person who spoke English whom they trusted to take care of the youth. The church leadership was looking for someone to take care of their teenagers and I was perceived as the right person because I spoke English and could be trusted to supervise young people."

The first six months on the job, no real Christian ministry happened. "We became successful because we had a gym downstairs. That gym turned into the center for the Ethiopian youth of Toronto. It brought young people together. For the kids playing in the gym downstairs, there was a strong sense of belonging there. The DNA of the Toronto Ethiopian community is connectedness." Running basketball outreach, organizing pizza nights, and bridging the gap between parents and kids, by the six months mark, Heskias and his leaders were packing the gym with youth, oftentimes fifty or sixty in an evening.

In the U.S., people move from one city to another city. But in Toronto, the majority of the people don't move. Youth grow up together. Most know each other for twenty or thirty plus years. So, the gym created a sense of community. "I definitely had a role in supporting this community, but I did not come in as a visionary leader who cast a vision which everyone followed. I fostered a community that already existed."

After six months, he introduced Christian programming. "We taught them how to sing, how to pray--they didn't even know Christian songs and they were in high school already! Maybe their parents were even elders! So, I developed the ministry, and something happened. A revival broke out! In late 2006 and 2007, the Spirit of God really moved. People started repenting of sins and encountering the Holy Spirit during camp meetings. Our community turned into a revival community. And our youth and young adult program kept growing.

"I was still working my IT job and I didn't have nearly enough time to do everything that needed to be done. So, I went to the elders, and I reported all that was going on. We had a young adult ministry, I said, an Amharic young adult ministry. We also had an English young adult ministry. And we had what should be called senior high ministry.

"I brought the elders a proposal. Going forward, I would not work with the youth. I asked them to assign the youth to a young man who had just graduated from Bible college, who would help me by working with the youth. I would mentor him, but I would focus on the over-eighteen people. They embraced my proposal and we hired Pastor Elias to run youth.

"At this point the church leadership had not considered breaking out these different types of ministry, which I believe illustrates the challenge facing the first-generation—no one had really grasped the second-generation needs. Today, in English, we have junior high, senior high, young adult and we've created a fourth group called Amharic-speaking Young Adults. (Young people coming from Ethiopia. They're in their twenties. You know, Amharic-speaking young adults)."

From 2008 to 2012, ministry boomed at the EECT, Heskias says. He attributes some of the church's growth in this period to its location by the subway stop and the strong sense of community among the youth. Young people flocked to the church, many initially for the gym but because the revival swept through, prayer and small groups flourished as well.

However, as the young adults aged, it was clear something new needed to happen. But what? The first-generation immigrant leaders were very much limited in understanding the millennial generation. Their own identities had been forged in the persecution after the Ethiopian military coup and fifteen years of Communist rule. They were forcibly scattered and became pioneers, building new lives in an English-speaking country. Their children, the millennials, seemed indecisive. After graduating from college many of the children moved back into their parents' basements. They were marrying later and since the pool of eligible mates in the Toronto Ethiopian community was limited, many who did marry married non-Ethiopians. First-generation leaders didn't think that their children were ready to make commitments and they couldn't be trusted to lead.

As these opinions gained strength among the parent generation, EECT Senior Pastor Zaharias heard about Tesfai Tesema and his plans for ministry to second-generation Ethiopians. In 2011, he invited Pastor Tesfai to come to Toronto to present his vision of a second-generation ministry to the Board.

When Heskias heard about the plan, he was doubtful. "I believed it would be a waste of everyone's time because

I believed no immigrant Ethiopian pastor understood the second-generation or even wanted to. When I met him, Pastor Tesfai looked like just another first-generation pastor. But two minutes into his presentation, I changed my mind. He was Habesha but he talked like my young adults! He told his story, how his sons had failed to connect with the Ethiopian Church he pastored and how that had driven him back to seminary to study the problem. He spoke intelligently about the problem. That was a surprise. He spoke Biblically—the story of the Church of Acts and cross-cultural ministry. For the first time I felt: we are not alone!"

Pastor Tesfai knew some of the elders in that room personally. They had come out of the church he <u>had founded in the Sudan in the 1980's</u> for refugee Ethiopians and Eritreans. He was already working with the Overflow Church in DC at this point, and he anticipated some of the objections they were going to raise. Tesfai made several simple recommendations to the elders of EECT:

- You have a strong English young adult ministry, and these young adults are passionate. Western Christians have great theology but many lack a real experience of salvation. Second-generation Ethiopians can connect with secular Canadians better than most North American Christians because they know the culture and language and because they are passionate about Christ! How might we enable them to reach out to Greater Toronto in ways you, as immigrants, cannot?

- Consider planting a second-generation church. You have a leader for the YA's who needs to be enabled and resourced. He's tent-making right now and that hobbles his ministry. He should be part of your Board decisions about the young adults because they are not only an important constituency in your church; they are the future of your church!
- If you decide to plant such a church, Pastor Tesfai said, I offer to act as a coach.

Heskias remembers what happened next. "We went out together to a Greek restaurant and the elders sat around and said: This is good. This is the first time we've thought about this idea. I was hopeful. I'd only been invited to Board meetings before when the youth broke something, or the police showed up. A second-generation church! I got excited! I began to believe Pastor Tesfai was a gift to our church!"

Unfortunately, the elders never called Pastor Tesfai back after that meeting to plan the next step. They continued to plod along, handling ministry for the young adults as before. Then the church moved buildings. The new church was a thirty-minute bus ride from the subway. In addition, the new building had no gym and the young adults only had access to the new building during hours when the congregation held Amharic services. No more hanging out. Attendance at the youth gatherings declined, dropping from fifty or sixty a night down to twenty, 'on nights when we were lucky.' People who had a heart for young adult ministry stayed on but those who had just come for community left.

"I was burnt out," Heskias says of this period, "preaching the same message over and over to my young adults. I knew our connections were strong, even if we looked disorganized to everyone else. We were a community. We cared about each other. I didn't consider leaving because they were my family. How can you leave family?"

In 2019, the youth pastor left, and the elders offered Heskias a fulltime pastor position and the opportunity to join the pastoral staff in regular meetings with the Board. He began to meet every week with the elders now. He sensed desperation among them, as they talked about keeping the next generation in the church. "We began talking together about a vision for the future. With their okay, I telephoned Pastor Tesfai.

"When I called, Pastor T expressed hope for Toronto. He was writing a book, he said, that he hoped might reopen the conversation we'd started years ago. He had a model of a successful second-generation ministry in Overflow Church in Washington, DC, he said.

"Something is happening," Heskias says today. "Maybe I can be a mouthpiece for it. This time things will be different!"

TWELVE

Minneapolis—the George Floyd Murder and Ebenezer

The intersection where Chicago Avenue crosses 38th Street in Minneapolis is not yet as well-known to Americans as Mount Rushmore or the Washington Monument. But this intersection, where black George Floyd died under the knee of white cop Derek Chauvin on May 25, 2020, has become hallowed ground to its visitors, just like Rushmore and the Monument.

On this sunny June evening, three weeks later, two artists are brush-painting a mural depicting Floyd on the side of the two-story brick building at the corner. They've completed Floyd's face, centering it on an enormous painted sunflower. They're blocking in Floyd's name in giant capitals that radiate both ways from his face, like the golden petals of the sunflower do. His eyes gaze out toward the intersection. The two streets seem strangely quiet because the police barricades have shut out all cars, for weeks now. In the center of the intersection, a ten-foot-high clenched fist, constructed of plywood painted copper, thrusts upward defiantly—the symbol of the Black Lives Matters movement. The spray-painted sign propped against the dais on which the fist was erected reads: THIS IS OUR COLLECTIVE PTSD. In a large circle around the fist sculpture, thousands of bouquets of flowers lie piled in one continuous river, most of them still in the transparent plastic sleeves they came in.

It feels a bit like a street faire out here tonight. The hundreds of visitors milling in the intersection walk and talk appropriately reverent. A pianist pounds jazz on a grand piano that sits, incongruously, in the middle of the street. A poet recites her rhymes into the standup mike on the sidewalk, to a circle of those who appreciate them. A shirtless man's hands dart back and forth in the smoke lifting from the charcoal Webber, turning hot dogs in various stages of grilling, while his partner distributes the dogs gratis, one by one, to the short queue. Overhead, the June sun sinks lower in the cloudless sky. George Floyd's painted eyes hold a look of surprise: What's happening here?

One block away and up the incline of Phelps Park, with a clear view of the intersection, a different event is going on. On the sun-bleached lawns halfway up, a cacophony of musical instruments sit in a row between two sound boxes that rest like black campfire marshmallows on top of their poles. The young man behind the full drum set of snare drums, cymbals, a bass, and a microphone leaning over them, is pounding furiously. The keyboardist goes self-conscious as the video camera turns her direction, lifts both hands in protest and shimmies her body in mock-protest.

Two singers, both Anglo, are crooning about the Most High.

Scattered downhill from the band, an audience of perhaps a hundred make clear that Most High should be capitalized. It's God they're singing to. They are an ethnically mixed group, but more Ethiopians than anyone else. Because coronavirus is raging across the country this summer, they 'social distance'—each standing somewhat awkwardly alone, six to eight feet apart from the next one. They sing along in various stances of worship. The twenty-something—(but then, aren't all of them twenty-something?)—in the tee shirt, with a tattoo (but don't all the guys wear tee shirts and sport tattoos?)—stretches his arms wide, like an NFL referee signaling a successful 3-point kick. The blonde with her long hair in dreadlocks holds up both hands with index fingers extended, as if she's stating a point, although her eyes are pinched shut. Her Covid mask hangs just off her chin, allowing her to sing about the One who loves like no one else.

The pastor smiles hugely and raises his arm as he passes the video camera. He pops up just his thumb and pinkie and waggles his hand surfer style. Like most in the crowd today, his black tee shirt carries a message:

I CAN'T BREATHE

George Floyd's dying words, as he lay on the pavement, with the officer's knee on his neck. He repeated them sixteen times over the eight minutes and forty-six seconds it took for the shutdown of blood up his carotid artery to his brain to kill him for lack of oxygen.

I CAN'T BREATHE. It's a solemn reminder of what this place is about.

Pastor Ebenezer walks to a spot uphill from the singers. The song dies and four of his leadership team come behind him to form a support line. Several of them are Ethiopian, like he is. One hands a microphone forward, which the pastor taps to make certain it's live.

"God really came through on the weather," Ebenezer says. Scattered downhill from him, some on steel folding chairs but most just sitting on the grass, 'socially distanced,' his audience puts their hands together to applaud the Almighty for the beautiful evening.

"We have three or four churches represented on the worship team tonight. Because we want to be church with a Capital C. We're coming together and saying, 'We're one body. We all believe in one God. We want to come together in unity and cry out to our Father and ask him to heal our land.'"

Afterward he would speak about what he felt as he stood there on the hillside, overlooking the memorial to George Floyd down the street. "People were just crying out to their God. And you could just feel that people wanted to see a move of God. People were hanging onto every word I was saying. That's not always the case, you know. So, it was refreshing to see people really desperate to hear God's word and desperate to see God's heart in all of this. I had conversations with our Anglo brothers and sisters afterward. I could tell they were hungry to learn. Like 'What can I do?

Who do I need to listen to? What's my part to play in all of this?'"

From down below, at the memorial intersection, someone leads the crowd in a call-and-response.

"Say his name!'

"George Floyd."

"Say his name!"

"GEORGE FLOYD!"

Pastor Ebenezer has more to say to his audience in Phelps Park and to those curious people in the intersection who have walked to the edge of the Park to look and see what's going on up the hill.

"Philippians," he says, and with one hand holding up his iPhone, he reads the text. "Chapter Two, one to four. Paul is making an argument for us to consider the interests of others. There's division within the Philippian community. They are already a persecuted church: the government is throwing followers of Jesus in prison; they're killing Christians. But there's also division within the church—two women have a disagreement and it's causing a division. Paul talks about that in Chapter Four. Hey! The world is already persecuting you. We need each other. 'If there's any encouragement from being united with Christ, if there's any comfort from his love.' God has made a way for us to be loved and to be united. We already have a world that's saying nasty things to each other on Facebook and Twitter. We have a world that's killing one another. We can't afford to do that within the church. This is a time for us to be one!"

After the worship in the Park, Ebenezer tells the back-story, what brought him here.

Four years ago, he says, a 32-year-old African American named Philando Castile was hailed by a St. Paul policeman, in a routine traffic stop that morphed into the policeman firing seven bullets into him, in front of the man's girlfriend and child. Philando died at Hennepin County Medical Center, the same hospital where they would take George Floyd by ambulance and pronounce him dead. The officer who shot Philando was charged with second-degree manslaughter and two counts of dangerous discharge of a firearm but after five days of deliberation, he was acquitted of all charges in a jury trial in 2017. Both the shooting and the acquittal led to large public demonstrations and outrage.

But Ebenezer felt no real remorse at the time. "When Philando was shot, my heart wasn't broken or torn. A lot of people thought my response was a problem. I didn't understand why. I had to take four years—from 2016 to the present, to do my homework. When I was ignorant, I didn't feel anything. But after four years of learning what's been happening and learning what God has to say about all of this—this time it really broke my heart.

"When I first saw the George Floyd video... oh, my tears! My anguish and turmoil! I couldn't eat! I couldn't think about anything else. For one week straight, here in the middle of Covid 19, the only time I felt at ease was when I went out to protest or came here to the memorial site. I couldn't sit at home. I felt broken, overwhelmed, heavy. My hope was being snuffed out of me, just like his breath was snuffed out. An Image-Bearer had his life taken from him.

"As I did my research after Philando, I realized something. All the pastors I had been listening to, all the podcasts, all the books—those were all white men talking. I had to start listening to black pastors, black podcasters, reading black authors. Because the white podcasters, authors and pastors weren't talking about events like police brutality. And the Ethiopian Church wasn't talking about them either.

"I put my head down. And I just read from people who knew what they were talking about because they were living out these events. I didn't just want a new perspective on this. I wanted a Biblical perspective on this. I had to ask people who I trusted to point me in the right direction. I had to look to Leonce Crumps and Ta-Nehisi and Pastor Charlie Dates. I read Martin Luther King. I even read Malcolm X. Growing up, I'd been taught he was this bad guy, this violent guy. When I read his story and watched the documentaries, I realized he wasn't about violence. He was about resistance.

"Someone asked Pastor Tim Keller a question the other week. They asked him, 'As you exegete our American culture, what is something the Church has to do to up its evangelism game?' And Keller said, "Justice! This generation—Gen Z, the millennials—they want to know what does God have to say about sex trafficking? What does God have to say about race relations? About pedophilia? We pastors can't just exegete the Biblical text. We have to exegete our culture as well.'"

Pastor Ebenezer grew up in Minnesota, the son of parents who moved here to pastor an Ethiopian Evangelical Church in 1994. He was two, which makes him a precocious twenty-nine-year-old pastor today.

"I'm totally Second-generation," Ebenezer says. "My parents moved to the suburbs to provide a better life for their kids. They wanted to provide opportunities for us to succeed. I'm grateful for that. But in a lot of ways, it confused me because I was a minority, and I didn't know who I was. I wasn't American enough for the Americans and I wasn't Ethiopian enough for the Ethiopians.

"Going to school every day, smelling like onions, for example. I always ended up the butt of jokes. And my house—why did it always smell like that? I felt nervous inviting friends over. I didn't want to get made fun of. Little things like that made me start resenting where I came from. It made me start questioning. Did God make a mistake when he made me Ethiopian? Let's get real personal. As a kid, I wanted to be white. I remember crying and asking my mom: how come we're not white? You know, it just came out of my confusion. She said 'No, everybody wants to be black.' And she would take me to the beach and show everybody getting a tan. 'See the color?' she would say."

In high school, Ebenezer became a Christ-follower. "Learning what Jesus or the Gospels had to say about who I was started me on a new journey. It wasn't until college that I started to get comfortable in my skin. I started to appreciate my heritage and my background.

"I felt the call at age fourteen. From an early age, I just had a heart to pastor. I know fourteen is young to decide what you want to do for the rest of your life!" The youth pastor at the Ethiopian Church discipled and mentored him. He had studied psychology as his undergraduate and then attended seminary at Oral Roberts University in Oklahoma. 'Study psychology,' the Youth Pastor told the young Ebenezer, "And I'll teach you how to read the Bible. The big benefit of seminary is learning the Greek and the Hebrew. But everything else, if you're disciplined, you can teach yourself,' he said. Seminary had given him tools and he now offered to pass on these tools to Ebenezer. 'Let me teach you how to fish and you go study psychology. Because ninety percent of your pastoral job they don't teach in seminary. How to relate with people, how to counsel people. Teaching is a very small piece of the job.'

Ebenezer took the Youth Pastor's advice and studied psychology at a Christian university, the University of Northwestern in St. Paul, and minored in Bible. He graduated in May of 2014 and in August of the same year, started work as a youth pastor in St. Louis. In 2016, his dad's church, the Ethiopian Evangelical Church of Minneapolis, hired him on as their youth pastor. The job was working with all the youth, everyone from age 13 to 25 gathered in one unmanageable meeting. His first task was figuring out a game plan for ministry to both groups. In 2016 the church split the youth and young adult ministry and after that the young adult ministry just started to grow.

"I mean, very quickly," Ebenezer recalls. "Young people were saying: This is a church that caters to me! It speaks my language! There are other young adults here! We can dive deep into the things of God as we talk about graduating college, marriage, kids, our vocations, what it looks like to honor God in culture. In this group we can articulate the heart of God as it relates to our lives. The group grew because of that. It also grew was because it was in English. Immediately we started to see it wasn't just Ethiopians and Eritreans coming to the young adult ministry. We had African-Americans coming. We had Caucasians coming. We had Hispanics and Asians."

Realizing the potential for growth led Ebenezer to another decision. "I knew if I stayed in the Ethiopian church, it would stunt my growth. Not just my growth but the growth of our Second-generation and 1.5's was at stake. The Ethiopian church was somewhat focused inward, due to the culture and language gap that existed. The First-generation couldn't reach our city or neighborhood in a way that maybe we could. We looked at the Word of God and we heard the call to the church to make disciples. We understood Ethiopians, but we also understood we were Americans. Owning both of those realities led to the birth of Perazim Church.

"Our mother church was completely supportive. They said: What do you guys need to get started? Just give us a budget. You can cast a vision for your group, raise leaders for your group, do whatever you want. We want to support you.

"That's how the conversation about a second-generation church began. We were blessed and fortunate to have leaders at Ethiopian Evangelical who believed in it. Most Ethiopian churches don't have a young adult ministry. Many churches are just now coming to see that they need a youth pastor. The leaders of Ethiopian Evangelical got more excited than I could have imagined. They supported us financially. They supported us with advice. They supported us with prayer, with resources. It took about a year and a half's worth of preparing. And then we launched.

"We call our church Perazim. It's Hebrew and it means 'God of the victory' or 'God of the breakthrough'. It's a really cool story in Second Samuel Five where David goes up against the Philistines and he prays to the Lord for victory. And the Lord said, I have given it to you. With that revelation, he goes and defeats the Philistines. So, he fights from the place of victory, not for the victory. We think that's a beautiful depiction of the gospel. On the cross, Jesus said It is finished. We engage in this life's battles knowing that He has defeated Sin.

"So that's our story. (We planted about a year ago. And we're trying to make the most of Covid 19. It's an interesting year to plant a church, I tell you.) There are over sixty thousand Ethiopians in the Twin Cities, and we have fourteen or fifteen Ethiopian churches. But we are the only Second Gen church!"

When people discover Ebenezer is an Ethiopian pastor interested in street justice and he's out protesting at the George Floyd Memorial Site, are they surprised?

"I think people in the world are surprised. Because the church has been silent for so long on issues of race relations and justice, it surprises them. When I talk to people who aren't Christians, there's this confusion. You Christians are about this? It shows how far removed we are from our history. When you look at Martin Luther King, Junior's legacy, I mean, he did everything through the church just a few short years ago. It seems like the church has lost its saltiness when it comes to the fight against injustice. I've seen people surprised that the church cares, that the church has something to say about this. I've also seen Christians surprised the other direction. Some Christians have pushed back on social media. I've gotten some nasty emails for speaking out on these issues.

"So, it's weird. There's the world that is bewildered and there are people in the Church (not our church), who are also bewildered. They think that we're being political, right? As if loving your neighbor is political. I just love how we politicize everything. We're now political if we wear a coronavirus mask. Some people think our fight for justice is a fight for vengeance. There's confusion over what is vengeance and what is justice. You're a pastor, not an activist, they say. Why are you speaking about these things? But Jesus spoke on these things. Look at the Good Samaritan. The thread of justice runs through the Old Testament, whether you're looking at Nehemiah or Amos or Esther. In story after story after story in the Old Testament, people fighting for justice. It just goes to show how far removed we are from really understanding the entirety of Scripture and what it teaches about justice.

"I've been thinking a lot about this. Indulge me for a few minutes! In the book of <u>Esther</u>, Esther is this Jewish woman thriving in the nation of Persia. By the grace of God, she's given the opportunity to live in a palace and she benefits from the palace. She benefits as the wife of a king. The crazy part comes when her people are sentenced to die because of Haman's decree. Esther doesn't see it as her problem. Because she lives in the palace.

"There's a parallel here with us, the Second-generation Ethiopians. We enjoy America. It's the palace, right? The promised land. Our parents sacrificed so much for us to have a bright future in this land. A better tomorrow. Access to education. Access to good paying jobs. When you think about America, you think Land of Opportunity.

"Mordecai tells Esther. Don't forget you are a Jew. You might be enjoying the palace. But this is coming for you, Esther. I apply this to myself and my fellow Ethiopians. Although we're not African-American, we're black. Martin Luther King said: 'A threat to justice anywhere is a threat to justice everywhere.' If we turn a blind eye to injustice falling on one group of people, it will come back to harm us.

"But something's upside down here. Us living in the palace, so to speak, and not caring about this fight our brothers and sisters are engaged in?

"My Youth Pastor used to say, as we were growing up: be responsible because—don't forget it!—you are replaceable.

God has given us gifts. God has given us opportunities. God has given us privilege. I not only have the privilege of birth in these United States, but I grew up in the United States and earned a college education. And my privilege is a responsibility. If I don't leverage these privileges, I am replaceable. If the Second-generation doesn't step up, the Kingdom of God will continue to advance. God will raise up somebody else. We will be replaced. If we don't choose to lean into this struggle—because this is the heartbeat of God—God will raise up somebody else. That's what Mordecai tells Esther."

"And lastly, he tells her, perhaps God has brought you to your royal position for such a time as this. Could it be that I was born and raised in America for such a time as this? Wow! That we planted Perazim Church in Minneapolis in the middle of everything that's going on for such a time as this? Could it be it's not a coincidence that all of this happened in our city?"

CONCLUSION

Our family friend runs a therapy business in Northern California. As you might expect, parents and children from Chinese, Korean, Indian (Asia), African and Filipino communities (to give a partial list), march into her office for counseling and they're often coming as a last result, when the family is fighting open warfare with each other.

They mostly come because they are fighting over respect, she says. The first-generation parent, feeling like an outsider and unfamiliar with the host society culture, responds with suspicion to the cultural norms of the new land and may be fearful. To protect his/her children, he attempts to force decisions on matters that his second-generation children consider should be theirs to make. He believes he must protect his children by asserting 'I know what is best for our family. Respect means you listen to me, just like I listened to my parents back in the Old Country.' Conflict soon bubbles up because the child, raised in this country, does not base his life on fear but independence. 'I would never do anything to deliberately hurt you, Parent. I respect your great sacrifices for our family. But you must acknowledge this is America and I have a right to make my own decisions.'

The immigrant teenager or young adult has a short list of demands that may run like this:

- I need space to figure out who I am without being told who I'm supposed to be.

- I appreciate everything you parents have done for our family, and I wish you'd done some things differently.
- I'm learning how to give myself permission, rather than seeking permission from someone older, and I may make choices my family may not agree with.
- I'm learning to differentiate between shame and guilt and just because I choose a certain path does not make me a bad daughter or son. (Even though I myself may wonder if I'm doing something wrong when I make the choice.)

I spent three years in Ft. Wayne, Indiana, from 2003–06, researching this question: *How do the Gen 1.5 and 2.0 immigrants from Ethiopia and Eritrea describe their identity? What are the implications of that for developing a culturally relevant ministry for them?* I interviewed 25 young Ethiopians and Eritreans by phone and in person, taped their responses and wrote my doctoral paper to answer this question. You will find a summary of these interviews in Chapter Seven of this book: 'Twenty-five Young Ethiopians Speak.' The participants in my study consistently described themselves as bicultural. They used words like 'Ethiopian-American,' 'American,' 'African-American.' Some called themselves 'Ethiopian' and some said 'African.' All of them self-identified as having one foot in America, one in the Old Country and they had no problem accepting themselves as 'American.'

First-generation parents and pastors must realize that what is attractive to their generation—the cultural setting of the first-generation, including the family and church—feels like a burden to their children. 'The very ambiance, including extensive formal and informal use of the native tongue, which seems the most attractive feature to the immigrant generation, alienates their Americanized offspring.'[92] This doesn't mean the children are rejecting their ethnicity. If anything, most of them are proud of their ethnicity. Nevertheless, the limits of that

home culture and the opportunity opening before them in their new country call them to relate to the culture differently than their parents have.

As I wrote in the Introduction, this is not unique to Immigrants from the Horn of Africa. My two sons do not limit their social world and circle of friends to people from their ethnic group, as is usual for the first-generation person. Together with other bicultural children of immigrants, Abel and Daniel attended the same elementary and high schools, speak the same English language and its slang, dance to the same music and watch the same movies and they share the same bicultural personality as these other bicultural children of immigrants, regardless of where in the world their Old Country was located. In fact—although this would be a topic for another book—they have more in common with the Anglo and African-American millennials of their generation than they have with people from their parent's generation, although these millennials may not share the one-foot-in-this-culture, one-foot-in-that-culture shadow on their personalities.

The U.S. is historically a land of immigrants, dramatically symbolized by the Statue of Liberty as she stands, welcoming, in New York Harbor. People started migrating to the United States four centuries ago. From 1620 to 1850, most immigrants came from Protestant Europe, Caucasian in ethnicity, with the notable exception of black Africans brought as slaves. From 1850 to 1950, Catholic populations, still European and Caucasian, came in large numbers, plus a small population of Chinese and Japanese.

My research and book describe the mostly non-white immigrants who came after the passing of the Civil Rights laws and the Immigration Act of 1965. By and large, these 'new immigrants' do not come from Europe. They are brown and black peoples. That means they face certain problems of assimilating into a race-conscious culture that the earlier immigrants from Europe perhaps did not face. My interviewees discuss that in Chapter Eight.

Research on these new immigrants tells us their children will likely not remain in the worship communities that their parents built and in which they grew up.

Karen Chai writes about second-generation Korean Protestant children. "... most 'grown up' second-generation Korean Americans do not attend their parent's church, even if they reside in the same city."[93] This phenomenon has received the designation "The Silent Exodus."[94] K.S. Yun writes, "Most second-generation Korean American college students abandon their church life when they enter college. ... More than 95% of the second-generation Koreans will be unchurched in a few years, making them one of the most unchurched people groups in the North American cities."[95]

My own experience as a pastor of an immigrant Ethiopian church in San Jose in the 1990s was this: the 1.5 and 2.0 generation young people left the church as soon as they graduated from high school. When it came to providing their children with 'a church of their own,' today it appears to me that many in the first-generation Ethiopian/Eritrean Christian leadership in North America are either in denial or they only reluctantly acknowledge this reality about their children. They also give very little support to the vision of planting a second-generation church.

The Bible offers guidance to the bicultural soul! Social realities like immigration, scattering and hybrid identities were no surprise to the Early Church. This generation too needs to see that their dispersion is not an accident. Seen through the eyes of faith, God has dispersed them for a purpose.

I believe 'the elect sojourner' addressed by St. Peter in 1 Peter 1:1, (which I describe in detail in Chapters Five and Six of this book) providentially gives more than guidance; it is a special identity. This sojourner identity very much predates the New Testament church. This motif or theme first appears with Abraham, who left the security of the Chaldean people and their sophisticated urban culture to become a blessing to the nations (Genesis 12:1–4), as he wandered in a Bedouin lifestyle, herding sheep and living in tents, from Syria to Egypt. The Apostle Paul would embrace a 'sojourner identity' which released him from the shackles of Jewish cultural idolatry and freed him to partner with God in the planting of churches where former pagan Gentiles and former ritual Jews would worship together.

In the same way, the 'elect sojourner' identity has life-changing implications for the Gen 1.5 and 2.0 Ethiopian Christian (and by extension, to the Gen 1.5 and 2.0 children of other people groups). God has a plan for your life that he expresses as he disperses you across the world. Embracing this 'destiny' frees you to a life committed to the Kingdom of God. It enables you to use culture, identity, and nationality for God's purposes, without being enslaved by them. Pledging ultimate allegiance only to God through Jesus Christ, you can avoid the tyranny of culture and live freely as a sojourner or global nomad. You are also freed from viewing yourself as a 'victim' of dispersion forced on you by hostile governments or armies or unjust laws.

Regarding missionary work or gospel outreach, the immigrant generation mostly limits its outreach to fellow ethnics, or mission work back in the Old Country. In contrast, the 1.5 and 2.0 generations move in a much larger social context, similar to the new Jewish believers in Christ in the New Testament city of Antioch. Their generation has an opportunity like that presented to Daniel and his friends (Daniel One). Offered the king's food and Babylon's pagan culture, they refused. Ultimately, Scripture says, Daniel and his friends 'shone like stars among the nations.' Gen 1.5 and 2.0 Ethiopians/Eritreans who claim their sojourner status in Christ will also shine like stars in the Ethiopian Diaspora.

This theological truth does more than give purpose to the immigrant son or daughter. One of the most powerful findings of my research is how faith in Christ as their core identity enabled several of my interviewees to successfully navigate identity formation and work out their conflicting social identities. My research speaks clearly to the value of faith in the lives of my interviewees. One young man described finding faith in Christ in his troubled and confusing adolescence years. 'Once I found my identity in Christ it was much easier to say I can relate with [others]. It really anchors you . . . I am a child of God. He formed me in His image. I do not have to be anything else, as long as I am right before him. I know my values now—Christian values.' This young man, now in his late twenties, helps other confused adolescents by mentoring immigrant kids in high school. His experience validates the critical need for the first-generation to establish strong English language Sunday Schools for children, youth groups for junior and senior highs and then a church of their own.

But what road map can we provide for the second-generation as they launch their own congregations? In the introduction of Chapter Five, I cited Fong's picturesque immigration timeline, which compares the social environment of people who are bicultural to fish swimming in a bay with many other bay fishes (think multiple ethnicities). However, in 2009, when I conducted my research, there were no such multicultural churches available anywhere in the Ethiopian community. So, in my research I focused on reporting results from other ethnic communities. From 2009 onward, a number of leaders have made courageous efforts to launch second-generation Ethiopian churches, with varying results. I tell four such stories in Part III of this book. The Overflow City Church story (Chapter Nine) inspires me! But we need more. Since America itself is growing increasingly multicultural, planting multicultural churches will not only benefit the children of immigrants but may also reach the host culture at its point of need.

Several options open to leaders as they consider the launch of a ministry to this population.

Option One – You live in a city with a large population of 1.5 and 2.0 Ethiopians. I'm thinking of major U. S. and Canadian cities like Washington DC, Seattle, Dallas, Minneapolis, Los Angeles, Houston, Chicago, Toronto and Vancouver. Here the strategy to pursue is an assimilationist multicultural church (see the Glossary) with the goal of becoming an integrated multicultural model. Initially the church targets ethnic Ethiopians but the mission of the church includes expansion to other immigrant communities, especially new immigrant communities of color.

Ken Uyeda Fong is a Third-Generation Chinese pastor who planted a church in Los Angeles. He and his team started by reaching out to the Chinese community. But because their outreach was in English and they are culturally American, they began to attract Korean youth as well, and then people from the neighborhood, including Caucasian and African-American non-immigrants. Gracepoint Church grew out of the University of California, Berkeley. Originally, their group was ethnically Korean, but the leadership has targeted the larger community and planted multicultural churches in other major college towns, like Washington DC and Los Angeles. These daughter churches are also becoming increasingly churches of multiple cultures.

Option Two – You live in a city with few 1.5 or 2.0 persons of your ethnicity. Collaborate with immigrant congregations of other ethnicities who have similar challenges with their 1.5 and 2.0 populations. This type of congregation starts as a pluralistic multicultural congregation with the goal of becoming an integrated multicultural church.

How does collaboration work? During research for my dissertation, I ran across an interesting idea called 'social capital,' an idea hatched by the University of Chicago, School of Business. Immigrants often lack 'social capital,' which means they lack connections to get capital to start a new business. The University encourages and helps immigrants through a process they call 'bonding and bridging,' to create their own credit union type bank and lend to themselves and so build their economic power in this country.

How would this work in a church launch setting? For us too, there's a social capital issue. A group of immigrant young people may not have a large enough population to pull off a church plant. In this instance, small, separate Ethiopian and Eritrean churches located in the same city might partner together to plant a second-generation English church. But why limit partnering to persons or churches of the same ethnic community? A "bonding and bridging" concept can forge a partnership between several ethnicities. For example, Ethiopians first bond with Ethiopians, Ghanaians bond with Ghanaians, Nigerians with Nigerians, and so on. You bond with culturally similar Christians. But then you bridge to another ethnic community to produce a larger good. By itself, neither small group has the wherewithal but together, they can do it. I do not have any good examples yet of a congregation that has started this way but it's a tool in the toolbox of the church planter.

These are some of the ideas I present when I conduct seminars. Typically, in the audience I will find both immigrant young people discontent in their parents' church and parents puzzled about the spiritual future of their children. I begin by affirming the young people's bi-culturalness. It's a special identity. The very fact that I affirm that identity comes as happy encouragement to the young people and new insight to the parents. The young adults sense permission to go plant a church of their own while I encourage the parents to think feel encouraged to think about legacy. For some, when I use Ken Uyeda Fong's picture of the river, the bay, and the ocean fish (see Chapter Five), a lightbulb flashes! For others, when I tell them the Esther and Mordecai story (Pages 174–175 of this book), it resonates with them. Like Esther, they're here **for such a time as this.** They could have a huge impact on their community, which includes the larger host society of the U.S. or Canada.

In fact, I am convinced the calling for the immigrant children is much grander than a call to plant 'their own church.' I'm getting excited here! I believe their call includes reviving evangelical Christianity in the Global North! It is a well-known fact that Christianity in North America and Europe is in decline. Research institutes like Pew have been writing with alarm that the number of religious 'nones,' the number of atheists and the followers of Eastern religions is mushrooming. The steady decline of Christianity is also observable by generations: More than eight-in-ten members of the Silent Generation (those born between 1928 and 1945) describe themselves as Christians (84%), as do three-quarters of Baby Boomers (76%). In stark contrast, only half of Millennials (49%) describe themselves as Christians; four-in-ten are religious "nones," and one-in-ten Millennials identify with non-Christian faiths. Some missiologists now label the West 'Post-Christian' and call for reconversion ("Can the West be converted?" See *The Princeton Papers*, by Bishop Lesslie Newbigin, 1984).

For the full Pew Forum 2019 survey, copy and paste this website into your browser: https://www.pewforum.org/2019/10/17/in-u-s-decline-of-christianity-continues-at-rapid-pace/.

In contrast with the spiritually cooling Northern Hemisphere, the Holy Spirit is multiplying white-hot churches in the Southern Hemisphere. In the last fifty years, the Christian faith has exploded in Africa, Latin America and Asia. For the first time in world history, more Christians live in the Global South than in the Global North. The election of Pope Francis from the Global South (Argentina) symbolizes the shift of the center of gravity for Christianity. I am convinced that the Church can mobilize the children of immigrants from the Global South, whose mission narrative and Christian experience is only that of incline and growth, as a God-sent gift to the Global North, to a people who in previous centuries had been faithful to the gospel but whose candle of faith now flickers erratically or perhaps looks like it's gone out because it's 'hiding under a bushel.'

And that's where I come in. As a leader and a pastor with outreach across North America, I sit with first-generation immigrant church pastors. I encourage them to set the stage for their children, to envision mobilizing the second-generation to preach the gospel to the host culture and people. I play the role of Mordecai in equipping the second-generation (Esthers) and call first-generation pastors to do the same as we embrace the elect sojourner identity in the land we now call home.

I get to sit with a fellow pastor and tell him: this is what is going on with your young people. That is why the relationship between Mordecai and Esther is a very, very helpful image for our times. She's dependent on him. But he is the one who encourages her to step out and he supports her when she does it. I see myself as that Mordecai, working to bridge both populations.

So, what is the purpose of this book I've written? It's much more than a call to plant second-generation churches for immigrant children. It's a vision that springs from my conviction that the scattering of immigrants from the Global South is God's providential plan to call the West back from its rejection of the Christian Faith.

There is your grand calling, Immigrant Child! Preach the good news of Jesus Christ to your neighbors in your adopted community, the Global North!

GLOSSARY

Abiy Ahmed Alian serves as the 10th Prime Minister of Ethiopia and the first ethnic Oromo chairman of the ruling Ethiopian People's Revolutionary Democratic Front (EPRDF). Abiy was awarded the 2019 Nobel Peace Prize for his work in ending the 20-year post-war territorial stalemate between Ethiopia and Eritrea.

Assimilation—Cultural assimilation is the process in which a minority group or culture comes to resemble a dominant group or assume the values, behaviors, and beliefs of another group.

Assimilation, Straight-line or Standard—a theory of how immigrants assimilate that proposes that each succeeding generation shows upward social mobility in education and occupation, integrating further into the American mainstream. This theory was especially successful in describing how immigrants from Europe in the 19th and early 20th Century assimilated into American culture.

Assimilation, Segmented—is the opposite of straight-line assimilation. This theory argues that starkly different outcomes are possible for the second-generation of immigration. Its members can end up "ascending into the ranks of a prosperous middle class or join in large numbers the ranks of a racialized, permanently impoverished population at the bottom of society." This theory became popular in the 1990s to describe the assimilation of the 'new immigrants' who came after 1965 and are mostly non-white.

Church model—Assimilationist multicultural church— (DeYoung, Emerson, Yancey and Kim, United by Faith, 2003) In the assimilated model, one ethnic group is obviously the dominant group within the congregation. This group's dominance is reflected in the worship services activities, and leadership. Congregation members who do not belong to the dominant ethnic group simply "assimilate" into the existing culture.

Church model—Pluralistic multiracial church—In this type of congregation, physical integration has occurred in the sense that members of different ethnic groups choose to gather in the same church and worship service. Although this physical integration is notable, members do not move beyond coexistence to real integration of social networks. While official committees may be multicultural, the informal social networks still remain segregated by ethnicity.

Church model—Integrated Multicultural Congregation— (DeYoung, Emerson, Yancey and Kim, *United by Faith*, 2003) This model of multicultural congregation is the ideal and the rarest of the three. This model is not accommodationist, where members of different races are encouraged to co-exist with their mosaic elements of separateness and distinct cultures. Rather, it aspires to create a hybrid of distinct cultures that have joined together in one church and one people. In other words, elements of distinct cultures are not incorporated to 'appease' diverse constituencies, rather, the new hybrid culture is an expression of the congregation's unified collective identity.

Diaspora—a Greek word that literally means: the scattering abroad. In the book of Acts, the concept is often translated as a verb. Acts 11:19—'now those who were scattered.' The apostle Peter uses the term to refer to the scattered believers in I Peter 1:1, where he addresses 'the exiles of the Diaspora (Dispersion).' 'Diaspora' has entered the English language and may be used to describe the scattering of any people, such as the Jewish Diaspora or the Ethiopian Diaspora.

Eastern Christianity—Church families that developed— outside of the West—from the original cradle of Christianity in Western Asia. Major bodies include the Eastern Orthodox Church, the Oriental Orthodox churches, the Eastern Catholic churches (that have re-established communion with Rome but still maintain Eastern liturgies) and Protestant Eastern Christian Churches, who are Protestant in theology but Eastern Christian in cultural practice. Ethiopian Protestants are an example of Eastern Christianity.

'Elect sojourner'—the term the Apostle Peter calls the scattered followers of Jesus in the English Standard Version

(ESV) translation. Dr. Bob Newton in the Foreword of this book makes the case that we should interpret Peter's words to mean God not only elected us to be His own but also chose us to be *strangers or exiles* in this world.

Eritrea is a country in Eastern Africa, with its capital at Asmara. It borders Sudan in the west, Ethiopia in the south, and Djibouti in the southeast. Eritrea is a multi-ethnic country, with nine recognized ethnic groups. The Kingdom of Aksum, covering much of modern-day Eritrea and northern Ethiopia, was established during the first or second centuries AD. During the 1890, Italy seized the territory, but it gained independence after Italy's defeat as an Axis power. In 1962, Ethiopia annexed Eritrea. In 1991, after 30 years of continuous armed struggle for independence, Eritrea became one of the newest African nations.

Ethiopia is a landlocked country in the Horn of Africa. It shares borders with Eritrea to the north, Djibouti to the northeast, Somalia to the east, Kenya to the south, South Sudan to the west and Sudan to the northwest. With over 109 million inhabitants as of 2019. Ethiopian national identity is grounded in the historic and contemporary roles of Christianity and Islam, and the independence of Ethiopia from foreign rule.

Ethiopian ethnic groups—Oromo, Amhara, Tigrai, Afar and Somali are the largest. All in all the Ethiopian Census lists more than 90 distinct ethnic groups. See Ethiopian-ness (below) for further information.

Ethiopian Orthodox Church—Ethiopia was the second country historically, following only Armenia, to officially proclaim Christianity as its state religion (in AD 333). Christianity became the established church of the Ethiopian Axumite Kingdom in the 4th century. The Church claims about 36 million members in Ethiopia, or 43.5% the country's population. The divine services of the Ethiopian Church are celebrated in the Ge'ez language, a liturgical language not used in ordinary conversation. There are many Ethiopian Orthodox churches located throughout the United States and other countries to which Ethiopians have migrated.

Ethiopian Protestants—Constitute 20% of the country's population. They are labeled P'ent'ays to indicate the prominence of the Pentecostal and charismatic nature of Ethiopian Evangelicalism. The major evangelical denominations in Ethiopia and Eritrea are General Baptist, Lutheran, Pentecostal, and Mennonite denominations

Ethiopian-ness—The country's population is highly diverse, containing over 90 different ethnic groups. According to the national census of 2007, the Oromo are the largest ethnic group in Ethiopia, at 34.4% of the nation's population. The Amhara represent 27.0% of the country's inhabitants, while Somalis and Tigrayans represent 6.2% and 6.1% of the population, respectively. In the 19th Century, the country's population was about nine million and grew to 109.5 million in 2018. Ethiopia has close historical ties with all three of the world's major Abrahamic religions—Christians constitute 62.1% of the population, Muslims 33.9% and Jews about 1%.

Ethnic Church—in the context of this book, an ethnic church is established to minister to the people of a particular Ethiopian or Eritrean people group. The language and culture of the church is the language and culture of that people group, for example, Amharic or Tigrinyan.

Ethnic/multi-ethnic—According to Talbot School of Theology, *Multi-ethnic* reflects most accurately the biblical concept of "the peoples" and it is the most helpful term when speaking about churches that are comprised of different families, clans, or cultural groups. Ethnicity is often a bigger determiner of a people's identity and worldview than race or nationality. Consider the fact that there may be many ethnicities that compose a single nationality, each with its own unique point of view.

Ge'ez is to Ethiopia as Latin is to the West. Ge'ez, like Latin, has not been used as a spoken language for a very long time. But like Latin, Ge'ez is the precursor of Ethiopia's three major Semitic languages. Ge'ez ceased to be used as a spoken language a short time before the tenth century CE. It is used today as the "liturgical language of the Ethiopian Orthodox

Church and was the only official written language of Ethiopia practically up to the end of the nineteenth century." (Hetzron)

Generation 1.0 or First-generation—According to the U.S. Census Bureau, a 'first-generation immigrant' refers to an immigrant, a foreign-born resident, who has relocated and become a citizen or permanent resident in a new country.

Gen 1.5—an individual who immigrated to a new country before or during their early teens. They earn the label the '1.5 generation' because they bring with them or maintain characteristics from their home country, meanwhile assimilating and socializing with their new country.

Gen 2.0 or Second-generation—In the U.S., this term refers to the U.S.-born children of foreign-born parents.

Global South—The Global South is an emerging term, used by the World Bank and other organizations, to identify countries on one side of the global North–South divide, the other side being the countries of the Global North. The Global South refers broadly to the regions of Latin America, Asia, Africa, and Oceania and is the area where the Christian church is growing most rapidly.

Habesha—Ethiopians and Eritreans use this term to refer to themselves. Most frequently, the term refers to Semitic language-speaking Christian peoples of highland Ethiopia and Eritrea but recently, some within diaspora communities use it to refer to all people of Eritrean or Ethiopian origin as Habesha. Habesha is a term of pride and may be used to eliminate the distinction between different tribes and celebrate unity as people of the same region.

Haile Selassie and Ethiopian Monarchy—Selassie (1892–1975) was the Emperor of Ethiopia from 1930 to 1974. He was a member of the Solomonic dynasty and traced his lineage to Emperor (10th Century, A.D.). Selassie is a defining figure in modern Ethiopian history. Among the Rastafari movement, Haile Selassie is still revered as the returned messiah of the Bible, God incarnate. Selassie was an Ethiopian Orthodox Christian throughout his life. The 1973 famine in Ethiopia led to his removal from the throne in 1975 at age 83, following a Marxist coup d'état.[96]

HUP or Homogeneous Unified Principle—a term developed and popularized by Donald A. McGavran the 1960s and 1970s. McGavran defined the HUP as: "The homogeneous unit is simply a section of society in which all the members have some characteristics in common." His work substantially changed the methods by which missionaries identify and prioritize groups of persons for missionary work and stimulated the Church Growth Movement.

'Kairos moment'—The Greeks used two different words to indicate time: *chronos,* which is used to indicate chronological or sequential time, and *kairos,* which are those moments of time we all desire and hope for. A **Kairos moment** in time is made up of three elements: **It is a moment of maximum opportunity. It is a moment when change is possible. It is a moment when all things "come together" and align.** In the Bible, Kairos is sometimes translated 'in the fullness of time' or 'at the acceptable time.'

Social capital—a concept coined by University of Chicago faculty, along with 'bonding and bridging.' Social capital defines the amount and quality of connections a person or group has. The immigrant often has little social capital and needs to link up with other immigrants to launch a business or a church. He 'bonds' with those like him and then reaches out or 'bridges' to those who are less similar.

The Derg—These low-ranking officers in the Ethiopian Army overthrew the government of the Ethiopian Empire and Emperor Haile Selassie during mass protests in 1974. The Derg abolished the monarchy and embraced communism as an ideology, establishing Ethiopia as a Marxist-Leninist one-party state. Mengistu Haile Mariam became Chairman in 1977 and launched the Red Terror to eliminate political opponents, imprisoning tens of thousands of Ethiopians without trial and executing them. In 1991, a coalition of rebel forces, the Ethiopian People's Revolutionary Democratic Front (EPRDF) overthrew Mengistu and has ruled continuously since then.

BIBLIOGRAPHY

Berry, John W. and Sam, David L. *Acculturation Psychology.* (New York: Cambridge University Press, 2006).

Britt, David: "From Homogeneity to Congruence," in *Planting and Growing Urban Churches: From Dream to Reality*, ed. Harvie M. Conn, Grand Rapids, MI: Baker Books.

Bruce, F. F. *Paul: Apostle of the Heart Set Free.* Grand Rapids, MI: Wm. B. Eerdmans Publishing Co., 2000.

_____ *The Epistles to the Colossians, to Philemon, and to the Ephesians. The New International Commentary on The New Testament.* Grand Rapids, MI: Wm. B. Eerdmans, 1991. (Reprinted)

Chacko, Elizabeth. "Identity and Assimilation among Young Ethiopian Immigrants in Metropolitan Washington." Geographical Review 93:4 (Oct 2003).

Chafetz, Janet Saltzman and Helen Ebaugh, *Religion and the New Immigrants: Continuities and Adaptations in Immigrant Congregations.* Walnut Creek, CA: Altamira Press, 2000.

Chai, Karen J. "Competing for the Second-generation: English-Language Ministry at a Korean Protestant Church," in Gatherings in Diaspora: Religious Communities and the New Immigration, ed. R. Stephen Warner and Judith G. Wittner (Philadelphia: Temple University Press, 1998), 300.

DeYoung, Curtiss Paul, Michael O. Emerson, George Yancey, Karen Chai Kim. *United by Faith: The Multiracial Congregation as an Answer to the Problem of Race.* New York: Oxford University Press, 2003.

Dubose, Francis M. *How Churches Grow in An Urban World.* Nashville, Tennessee: Broadman Press, 1978.

Earle, Ralph. *Word Meanings in The New Testament.* Grand Rapids, MI: Baker Book House, 1989. (Fifth Printing)

Emerson, Michael O., and Christian Smith. *Divided by Faith: Evangelical Religion and the Problem of Race in America.* New York: Oxford University Press, 2000.

Fairbairn, Donald. *Eastern Orthodoxy Through Western Eyes.* Louisville, KY: Westminister John Knox Press, 2002.

Fong, Ken Uyeda. *Pursuing the Pearl: A Comprehensive Resource for Multi-Asian Ministry.* Valley Forge, Pa: Judson Press, 1999.

Foster, Mary, Agnes Meinhard, and Ida Berger. *The Role of Social Capital: Bridging, Bonding or Both?* Toronto, Canada: Ryerson University Faculty of Business. http://www.ryerson.ca/cvss/work.html.

Grudem, Wayne. *1 Peter.* Tyndale New Testament Commentaries. Grand Rapids, MI: William B. Eerdmans, 1988.

Hays, Richard B. *The Moral Vision of the New Testament.* San Francisco: Harper, 1996.

Kim, Henry H., and Ralph E. Pyle. An Exception to the Exception: Second-Generation Korean American Church Participation. Social Compass 51:321 (2004).

Kittel, Gerhard, Gerhard Friedrich, and Geoffrey William Bromiley. *Theological Dictionary of the New Testament: Abridged in*

One Volume. Grand Rapids, MI: W.B. Eerdmans, 1985.

Ladd, George Eldon. *A Theology of The New Testament*, rev. ed. (Grand Rapids, MI: William Eerdmans, 1993).

McGavran, Donald A. *Understanding Church Growth.* Grand Rapids, MI: William B. Eerdmans, 1990.

_____ Effective Evangelism: A Theological Mandate. Phillipsburg, New Jersey: Presbyterian and Reformed Publishing Company, 1988.

_____ *"Why Some American Churches are Growing and Some are Not,"* in Elmer L Towns, John N Vaughan and David J. Seifert, editors. *The Complete Book of Church Growth*. (Wheaton, IL: Tyndale House, 1981).

Newton, Robert. "Drop the Comma: A Transformed Vision of Who We Are," in *Missional Transformation: God's Spirit at Work*. Essays Celebrating the Outreach Ministry of Dr. Eugene Bunkowske. Ed. by Mark G. Press and Eugene W. Bunkowske. AuthorHouse, Bloomington, IN, 2012.

Newbigin, Lesslie. "Can the West be Converted?" Based on the Warfield Lectures at Princeton Theological Seminary. Published in the International Bulletin of Mission Research, 1987.

NIV Bible Works for Windows 98/2000 release. Copyright © 2001 Bible Works, LLC Version 5.0.020

Pew Forum Research, 2019. "In U.S., Decline of Christianity Continues at Rapid Pace: An update on America's changing religious landscape." https://www.pewforum.org/2019/10/17/in-u-s-decline-of-christianity-continues-at-rapid-pace/

Rhodes, Stephen A. *Where the Nations Meet: The Church in a Multicultural World*. Downers Grove, Illinois: InterVarsity Press 1998

Smith, James Clapsaddle. *Without Crossing Barriers: The Homogenous Unit Principle in The Writings of Donald McGavran*. Ann Arbor, Michigan: U.M.I Dissertation Services, 1981.

Stott, John R. W. *The Message of Acts*. Downers Grove, IL: InterVarsity Press, 1990.

Suarez-Orozco, Carola, and Marcelo M. Suarez-Orozco. *Children of Immigration*. Cambridge, MA: Harvard University Press, 2001.

Van Engen, Charles. God's Missionary People. Grand Rapids, MI: Baker Book House, 1997. (Fourth Printing)

_____ *Mission on the Way*. 2nd ed. Grand Rapids, MI: Baker Books, 2000.

_____ "Is the Church for Everyone? Planting Multi-Ethnic Congregations in North America." *Journal of the American Society for Church Growth* 11 (Spring 2000).

Vine, W. E. *Vine's Expository Dictionary of The Old and New Testament*. Old Tappan, NJ: Fleming H. Revell Company, 1981.

Wagner, Peter. "Strategy for Urban Evangelism," Chicago: Moody: Frontiers in Mission Strategy 1971).

_____ *Our Kind of People: The Ethical Dimensions of Church Growth in America*. (John Knox: Atlanta, GA 1979)

_____ Church *Growth and the Whole Gospel: A Biblical Mandate*. (Harper & Row. New York, NY 1981).

Waters, Mary C. *Ethnic Options: Choosing Identities in America*. Berkeley and Los Angeles, CA: University of California Press, 1990.

Yun, Young Shik. "Dualism and the Worldview of Second-Generation Korean American College Students." Ph.D. diss. Fort Wayne, IN: Concordia Theological Seminary, 2006.

ENDNOTES

1   "Drop the Comma: A Transformed Vision of Who We Are," in *Missional Transformation: God's Spirit at Work. Essays Celebrating the Outreach Ministry of Dr. Eugene Bunkowske.* Ed. by Mark G. Press and Eugene W. Bunkowske. AuthorHouse, Bloomington, IN, 2012. pp. 178-194.

2   KJV: Peter, an apostle of Jesus Christ, to the strangers scattered throughout Pontus, Galatia, Cappadocia, Asia, and Bithynia. Elect according to the foreknowledge of God the Father ...

    RSV: Peter, an apostle of Jesus Christ, to the exiles of the Dispersion in Pontus, Galatia, Cappadocia, Asia, and Bithynia, chosen and destined by God the Father ...

    NASB: Peter, an apostle of Jesus Christ, to those who reside as aliens, scattered throughout Pontus, Galatia, Cappadocia, Asia, and Bithynia, who are chosen according to the foreknowledge of God the Father ...

3   C. Wagner, Peter. "Strategy for Urban Evangelism," Chicago: Moody: Frontiers in Mission Strategy 1971) 194.

4   All English Bible texts are taken from the NIV version of the Bible Works for Windows 98/2000 release. Copyright © 2001 Bible Works, LLC Version 5.0.020w

5   John R. W. Stott, *The Message of Acts*, (Downers Grove, IL: Inter-Varsity Press, 1990), 63.

6   Curtiss Paul DeYoung, Michael O. Emerson, George Yancey, Karn Chai Kim, *United by Faith: The Multiracial Congregation as an Answer to the Problem of Race*, (New York, NY: Oxford University Press, 2003), 22.

7   Francis M. DuBose, *How Churches Grow in an Urban World*, (Nashville, TN: Broadman Press, 1978), 127.

8   Stott, *The Message of Acts*, 120.

9   Stott, *The Message of Acts*, 126.

10   DeYoung et al, *United by Faith*, 23.

11   The experience called "dispersion" or "scattering" which Luke calls attention to, was crucial to the spread of Christianity. I see this same phenomenon at work among 1.5 and 2.0 Ethiopian Christians. This important theological factor needs special attention, which we will address later in this Biblical section.

12   Stott, *The Message of Acts*, 203.

13   Ralph Earle, *Word Meanings in the New Testament*, (Grand Rapids, MI: Baker Book House, 1989), 107.

14   Stott, *The Message of Acts*, 202.

15   F. F. Bruce, *Paul: Apostle of the Heart Set Free*, (Grand Rapids, MI: William B. Eerdmans, 2000), 131.

16   Bruce, *Paul: Apostle of the Heart Set Free*, 133.

17   Stott, *The Message of Acts*, 205.

18   Earle, *Word Meanings in the New Testament*, 108.

19   DeYoung et al, *United by Faith*, 29.

[20] Ibid., 29-30.

[21] Ibid., 31

[22] Bible Works 5 Software. Greek and Hebrew Lexicon.

[23] Ibid.

[24] Kittel, Gerhard, Gerhard Friedrich, and Geoffrey William Bromiley, *Theological Dictionary of the New Testament: Abridged in One Volume*, (Grand Rapids, MI: W.B. Eerdmans, 1985), 1048-9.

[25] *Vines Expository Dictionary of the Old and New Testament*, Volume 2: E-LI. 21

[26] Kittel et al, *TDNT*, 149.

[27] Wayne Grudem, *1 Peter*, Tyndale New Testament Commentaries, (Grand Rapids, MI: William B. Eerdmans,) 48.

[28] Ibid.

[29] Ibid.

[30] Grudem, *1 Peter*, 48.

[31] Kittel et al, *TDNT*, 157

[32] Grudem, *1 Peter*, 49.

[33] Ibid.

[34] George Eldon Ladd, *A Theology of The New Testament*, rev. ed. (Grand Rapids, MI: William Eerdmans, 1993), 641.

[35] Stephen A. Rhodes, *Where the Nations Meet: The Church in a Multicultural World*. (Downers Grove, IL: InterVarsity Press, 1998), 25-6.

[36] Ladd, *A Theology of The New Testament*, 94.

[37] Ladd, *A Theology of The New Testament*, 94.

[38] Richard B. Hays, *The Moral Vision of the New Testament: Contemporary Introduction to New Testament Ethics*, (San Francisco, CA: Harper Collins Publishers, 1996), 108.

[39] Van Engen. *"Is the Church for Everyone? Planting Multi-Ethnic Congregations in North America."* Journal of the American Society for Church Growth (ASCG) - Volume 11 - Spring 2000, 14

[40] Donald A. McGavran, *Understanding Church Growth*, (Grand Rapids, MI: W.B. Eerdmans, 1990), 95.

[41] McGavran, *Understanding Church Growth*, 97.

[42] Ibid., 223.

[43] James Clapsaddle Smith, *Without Crossing Barriers: The Homogeneous Unit Concept in the Writings of Donald McGavran.* (Ann Arbor, Michigan: U.M.I Dissertation Services, 1976) 90.

[44] C. Wagner, Peter. "Strategy for Urban Evangelism," Chicago: Moody: Frontiers in Mission Strategy 1971) 194.

[45] C. Wagner, Peter. *Our Kind of People: The Ethical Dimensions of Church Growth in America.* (John Knox: Atlanta, GA 1979) 11

[46] McGavran, Donald A. *"Why Some American Churches are Growing and Some are Not,"* in Elmer L Towns, John N Vaughan and David J. Seifert, editors. *The Complete Book of Church Growth.* (Wheaton, IL: Tyndale House, 1981) 290-294.

47 Donald A McGavran, *Understanding Church Growth*, 226.

48 Wagner, Peter C. *Church Growth and the Whole Gospel: A Biblical Mandate*. (Harper & Row. New York, NY 1981) 166-167.

49 Ibid., 167

50 Wagner, Peter C. *Church Growth and the Whole Gospel: A Biblical Mandate* 167-8

51 Donald A McGavran, *Understanding Church Growth*, 244

52 Ibid., 241.

53 Ibid., 238.

54 Van Engen, Charles. *"Is the Church for Everyone? Planting Multi-Ethnic Congregations in North America,"* 41

55 Ibid., 41-2

56 Van Engen, Charles. *"Is the Church for Everyone? Planting Multi-Ethnic Congregations in North America."* 41

57 Ibid., 41-2

58 Van Engen, Charles. *"Is the Church for Everyone? Planting Multi-Ethnic Congregations in North America."* 26

59 Ibid., 26

60 Van Engen, Charles. *"Is the Church for Everyone? Planting Multi-Ethnic Congregations in North America."* 26-7

61 Smith, James Clapsaddle. *Without Crossing Barrier*, 110.

62 Ibid.

[63] Smith, James Clapsaddle. *Without Crossing Barrier*, 110

[64] Francis M Dubose, *How Churches Grow in an Urban World* (Nashville, Tennessee: Broadman Press 1978) 123.

[65] Michael Emerson and Christian Smith, *Divided by Faith: Evangelical Religion and the Problem of Race in America*, (New York: Oxford University Press, 2000), 155-6.

[66] David Britt, "From Homogeneity to Congruence," in *Planting and Growing Urban Churches: From Dream to Reality*, ed. Harvie M. Conn, (Grand Rapids, MI: Baker Books,), 137-8.

[67] F. F. Bruce, *the Epistles to the Colossians, to Philemon, and to the Ephesians*, the New International Commentary on New Testament (Grand Rapids, MI: William B. Eerdmans, 1991), 295-6.

[68] Charles Van Engen, *God's Missionary People: Rethinking the Purpose of the Local Church*. (Grand Rapids, MI: Baker Book House, 1997), 56.

[69] Donald Fairbairn, *Eastern Orthodoxy through Western Eyes*, (Louisville, KY: Westminster John Knox Press, 2002), 143.

[70] As Fairbairn traces the history of religious nationalism, he points out that "during the Western Middle Ages and the Byzantine period in the East, nationalism was (to some degree) held in check by the larger political and social units.

[71] Ibid.

[72] Ibid.

[73] Ibid., 145-6

[74] Ibid., 144.

75 Ibid., 145.

76 Ibid., 146.

77 Ibid., 146-7.

78 Curtiss Paul DeYoung, Michael O. Emerson, George Yancey, Karn Chai Kim, *United by Faith: The Multiracial Congregation as an Answer to the Problem of Race*, (New York, NY: Oxford University Press, 2003), 165.

79 Ibid., 165

80 Ibid., 167.

81 Ibid., 168.

82 Ken Uyeda Fong, *Pursuing the Pearl: A Comprehensive Resource for Multi-Asian Ministry*. (Valley Forge, Pa: Judson Press, 1999), 205.

83 Ibid., 211.

84 Orozco, Carola S and Orozco, Marcelo S. *Children of Immigration*. (Cambridge: Harvard University Press, 2002), 135.

85 Orozco, Carola S and Orozco, Marcelo S. *Children of Immigration*, 137.

86 Waters, Mary. *Ethnic Options: Choosing Identities in America*. Berkeley and Los Angeles, CA: University of California Press, 1990, 102.

87 Suarez-Orozco Carola and Suarez-Orozco, Marcelo M. *Children of Immigration*. (Cambridge: Harvard University Press, 2001), 73–74.

[88] Ibid, page 73. A form of stress specific to immigration is referred to as "acculturation stress." Acculturation is the process of learning new cultural rules and interpersonal expectations. Language is not the only form of communication that immigrants must learn.

[89] Chacko, Elizabeth. *"Identity and Assimilation among Young Ethiopian Immigrants in the Metropolitan Washington,"* 5.

[90] Ibid, 6.

[91] Berry John W. and Sam David L. *Acculturation Psychology.* (New York: Cambridge University Press, 2006), 81.

[92] Chafetz, Janet S. and Ebaugh Helen R. *Religion and the New Immigrants*, page 430.

[93] Karen J. Chai, "Competing for the Second-generation: English-Language Ministry at a Korean Protestant Church," in Gatherings in Diaspora: Religious Communities and the New Immigration, ed. R. Stephen Warner and Judith G. Wittner (Philadelphia: Temple University Press, 1998), 300.

[94] Young Shik Yun, "Dualism and the Worldview of Second-Generation Korean American College Students," (Ph.D. diss., Concordia Theological Seminary, 2006), 39.

[95] Ibid.

[96] Oromo children's books keep once-banned Ethiopian language alive, 13 February 2016, retrieved 14 February 2016 per Wikipedia.

Made in the USA
Monee, IL
14 April 2022